STOIC TENNIS

365 DAILY MEDITATIONS FOR THE BASELINE AND BEYOND

EROCH CHRYSANDROS TOLUCA

Copyright © 2025 by Eroch Chrysandros Toluca.

ISBN: 979-8-218-68166-1

All rights reserved. No part of this book may be reproduced or transmitted in any form or by any means, electronic or mechanical, including photocopying, recording, or by any information storage and retrieval system, without permission in writing from the copyright owner.

Contents

Author's Statement 7

Introduction 9

Why Stoicism? 11

The Stoic Tennis Player 12

The Daily Practice 13

Beyond the Court 14

The Path Ahead 15

January: The Foundation – Building Mental Toughness 17

January Wrap-Up 49

February: Passions and Emotions – Mastering Your Inner World 51

February Wrap-Up 81

March Introduction: The Obstacle Is the Way – Turning Adversity Into Advantage 83

March Wrap-Up 115

April Theme: Stoic Clarity — Mastering Perception and the Power of Thought 117

April Wrap-Up 148

May Theme: Virtue in Action — Building Character On and
    Off the Court 151

May Wrap-Up 183

June Theme: Resilience and Endurance — Weathering the
    Storms 185

June Wrap-Up 216

July Theme: Community, Friendship, and the Common
    Good — The Stoic Team Spirit 219

July Wrap-Up: Playing with Integrity and Respect 251

August Theme: Emotional Mastery — Stoic Calm in the
    Heat of Competition 253

September Theme: The Virtue of Curiosity — Lifelong
    Learning On and Off the Court 287

September Wrap-Up: Strategic Thinking — Wisdom
    Between the Lines 318

October: The Discipline of Purpose – Aligning Action
    with Values 321

October Wrap-Up: Tennis by Design 353

November Theme: The Virtue of Generosity — Giving and
    Growing Through Tennis 355

November Wrap-Up: The Virtue of Generosity — Giving
    and Growing Through Tennis 386

December Theme: The Virtue of Reflection — Wisdom Gained, Lessons Carried Forward..389

December Wrap-Up: The Virtue of Reflection — Wisdom Gained, Lessons Carried Forward...421

Author's Statement
WHY I CREATED THIS BOOK

I WROTE THIS BOOK not as a master of Stoic philosophy, but as a humble student — someone still learning, still stumbling, and still striving to apply these ancient lessons both on and off the tennis court. My journey with Stoicism began as a way to better handle the frustrations, setbacks, and emotional swings that come with playing tennis, but it quickly grew into something much deeper: a daily practice for living with more resilience, clarity, and joy.

Tennis, for me, has always been more than a game. It's a lifelong classroom where every match, every point, and every mistake offers a lesson in character.

I am still learning to embody Stoic principles — accepting what I can't control, responding to adversity with calm, and finding meaning in the process rather than the outcome. I often fall short, but I believe that sharing this journey, with all its imperfections, might help others who are also seeking a steadier mind and a fuller experience of the game.

This book is my attempt to pass along what I've learned (and am still learning): that tennis, like life, is unpredictable and sometimes unfair, but always offers us a chance to grow. If these daily reflections help you find a little more patience, perspective, or joy — on the court or beyond — then I will consider this project a success. We are all students, and the court is always open for another lesson.

Introduction

THE STOIC COURT — WHERE ANCIENT WISDOM MEETS MODERN TENNIS

TENNIS IS MORE than a game of physical skill — it's a mental battlefield. Every match tests not just your forehand or serve, but your ability to stay calm under pressure, adapt to adversity, and maintain focus amid chaos. For centuries, athletes, warriors, and leaders have turned to Stoic philosophy to master these very challenges. This book bridges the gap between ancient wisdom and modern tennis, showing how Stoic principles — practiced by thinkers like Marcus Aurelius, Epictetus, and Seneca — can transform your game, your mindset, and your life.

Why Stoicism?

STOICISM, BORN IN ancient Greece and Rome, is a philosophy of resilience, clarity, and self-mastery. Its core tenets — focusing on what you control, reframing obstacles as opportunities, and cultivating unshakable inner peace — are strikingly relevant to tennis.

Stoicism teaches that external events are neutral; it's our judgments about them that create suffering or strength. In tennis, this means shifting from "Why is this happening to me?" to "How can I use this to grow?"

The Stoic Tennis Player

Great players aren't born — they're forged through disciplined thought and action. This book is structured as a daily guide because Stoicism, like tennis, is a practice. Each day, you'll pair a Stoic lesson with actionable tennis wisdom, building habits that compound over time.

Here's how Stoic virtues align with the demands of the court:

1. **Courage:** Not the absence of fear, but the will to act despite it.

2. **Wisdom:** Seeing situations clearly and responding rationally.

3. **Temperance:** Mastering impulses and emotions.

4. **Justice:** Respect for the game, opponents, and oneself.

The Daily Practice

THIS BOOK IS designed as a year-long journey because transformation happens incrementally. Each entry includes:

- **A Stoic Quote:** Timeless wisdom from philosophers, athletes, and thinkers.

- **Tennis Interpretation:** How to apply the lesson to your game, from managing nerves to refining technique.

- **Actionable Insight:** A simple, concrete step to embed the principle into your practice.

For example, Epictetus' teaching — "It's not what happens, but how you react that matters" — translates to resetting after a missed shot by focusing on the next point, not the error. Seneca's warning — "We suffer more in imagination than reality" — becomes a tool to quiet pre-match anxiety by grounding yourself in preparation, not hypothetical disasters.

Beyond the Court

WHILE THIS BOOK focuses on tennis, Stoicism's lessons extend far beyond it. The mental toughness you build here — grace under pressure, resilience in failure, joy in the process — will serve you in relationships, careers, and personal challenges. Tennis becomes a metaphor for life: a series of points to play, not outcomes to fear.

How to Use This Book

1. **Read daily:** Start each morning with an entry to set your mindset.

2. **Reflect:** Journal how the lesson applies to recent matches or struggles.

3. **Act:** Implement the "Actionable Insight" deliberately in practice.

4. **Repeat:** Return to key entries when facing specific challenges (e.g., handling anger or rebuilding confidence).

The Path Ahead

TENNIS, LIKE LIFE, is unpredictable. But with Stoicism as your foundation, you'll learn to thrive in uncertainty. Whether you're a junior player, a weekend competitor, or a seasoned pro, this book offers a roadmap to:

- Play freely, unburdened by fear of failure.

- Grow relentlessly, using every obstacle as fuel.

- Compete with integrity, knowing your character matters more than any trophy.

The Stoics remind us that excellence is not a destination, but a daily practice. Let this book be your guide to mastering the inner game — the one that ultimately determines success on the court and beyond.

> "The impediment to action advances action. What stands in the way becomes the way."
> — MARCUS AURELIUS

Welcome to a year of growth, resilience, and transformation. The court awaits.

January

The Foundation – Building Mental Toughness

January is about laying the groundwork for your tennis journey by developing mental toughness. This month, you'll focus on building resilience, managing emotions, and controlling your mindset — skills that help you stay composed and perform your best under pressure. Each day offers a Stoic principle and practical advice to strengthen your mental game and set the stage for lasting growth, both on and off the court.

January 1
CONTROL WHAT YOU CAN

> "You have power over your mind — not outside events. Realize this, and you will find strength."
>
> — Marcus Aurelius

In tennis, you can't control your opponent's skill, the weather, or bad line calls. However, you can control your attitude, focus, and effort. Strength comes from letting go of what's outside your control and channeling your energy into what truly matters — your performance. By focusing on what you can control, you maintain mental toughness and resilience. This mindset helps you stay calm and composed even in the face of adversity.

 Actionable Insight: During your next match, repeat this mantra when frustration arises: "Focus on what I can control." Practice staying calm in the face of external distractions.

January 2
THE POWER OF PREPARATION

> "Luck is what happens when preparation meets opportunity."
> — SENECA

Winning isn't about luck — it's about being prepared when opportunities arise. Whether it's a break point or a crucial tiebreaker, success depends on the work you've done beforehand. Preparation in practice builds confidence and ensures you're ready for high-pressure moments. By focusing on preparation, you set yourself up for success and reduce reliance on chance. This mindset also helps you stay motivated and disciplined in your training.

Actionable Insight: Identify one area of your game that needs improvement (e.g., volleys) and dedicate extra time to it this week. Trust that preparation will pay off in matches.

January 3
MASTER YOUR REACTIONS

> "Man is affected not by events but by the view he takes of them."
>
> — Epictetus

A bad call or an opponent's lucky shot doesn't ruin a match — your reaction to it does. By reframing setbacks as challenges rather than obstacles, you maintain control over your emotions and performance. A calm mind allows you to stay focused and play your best tennis. This ability to manage your reactions is crucial for maintaining momentum and staying in the zone during matches. It also helps prevent emotional exhaustion and keeps you fresh for the next point.

 Actionable Insight: During practice matches, simulate frustrating scenarios and train yourself to respond calmly rather than emotionally.

January 4
SMALL WINS LEAD TO BIG VICTORIES

> "Well-being is realized by small steps, but it is no small thing."
>
> — Zeno of Citium

Matches are won one point at a time. Instead of focusing on the final score, concentrate on winning each individual point through consistent effort and focus. Small victories build momentum and lead to greater success over time. Celebrating these small wins keeps you motivated and helps you stay present in the match. By focusing on one point at a time, you reduce pressure and perform more naturally.

 Actionable Insight: Break your next match into smaller goals (e.g., "Win this game" or "Make my first serve"). Celebrate each small win as progress toward the larger goal.

January 5
ADVERSITY BUILDS STRENGTH

> "The impediment to action advances action. What stands in the way becomes the way."
>
> – MARCUS AURELIUS

Tough opponents or challenging conditions aren't obstacles — they're opportunities to grow stronger. Adversity forces you to adapt and improve, making you a more resilient player. Embracing difficulties as essential parts of your journey toward mastery helps you develop strategic thinking and mental toughness. This mindset also fosters a growth mindset, where challenges are seen as stepping stones to success rather than barriers. By embracing adversity, you become more adaptable and resourceful on the court.

Actionable Insight: Seek out players who are better than you for practice matches this week. Reflect on what you learned from these challenges afterward.

January 6
FOCUS ON EFFORT OVER OUTCOME

"We suffer more often in imagination than in reality."
— SENECA

Worrying about losing distracts you from playing your best tennis in the present moment. Instead of fixating on outcomes, focus on giving maximum effort during each point. Letting go of imagined fears allows you to perform with clarity and confidence. This mindset helps you stay present and focused on what you can control — your effort and attitude. By focusing on effort, you reduce anxiety and improve your overall performance.

Actionable Insight: Set an effort-based goal for your next match (e.g., "I'll hustle for every ball" or "I'll stay positive no matter what"). Measure success by how well you stick to this goal.

January 7
THE IMPORTANCE OF REST

"If you seek tranquility, do less."

— Marcus Aurelius

Improvement requires rest as much as it requires effort. Overtraining leads to burnout and injury; taking time off allows your body and mind to recover so you can come back stronger. Rest isn't laziness — it's an essential part of growth, allowing your muscles to repair and your mind to recharge. Proper rest also helps prevent mental fatigue, ensuring you stay motivated and focused during training. By embracing rest, you maintain a healthy balance between work and recovery.

 Actionable Insight: Schedule at least one rest day this week where you step away from tennis entirely. Use this time to reflect on your goals or simply recharge.

January 8
PATIENCE IS POWER

> "No great thing is created suddenly."
>
> — EPICTETUS

Improvement in tennis takes time, whether it's mastering a new stroke or building mental toughness. Rushing the process often leads to frustration and mistakes, but patience allows you to focus on steady progress. Long rallies or tough matches are tests of your ability to stay calm and wait for the right moment to strike. By embracing patience, you develop discipline and confidence in your ability to persevere. This mindset not only improves your game but also helps you enjoy the journey of growth.

Actionable Insight: During your next match, focus on staying patient during long rallies. Remind yourself to wait for the right opportunity to attack instead of forcing risky shots.

January 9
CONTROL YOUR EMOTIONS

> "Anyone can get angry — that is easy. But to be angry with the right person, to the right degree, at the right time, for the right purpose, and in the right way — that is not easy."
>
> — Aristotle

Anger after a missed shot or frustration with an opponent can quickly derail your focus if left unchecked. Emotional control is one of the most important skills a tennis player can develop — it allows you to stay composed and make clear decisions under pressure. Instead of letting emotions control you, channel them into productive energy that fuels your performance. This doesn't mean suppressing emotions but rather managing them effectively so they don't interfere with your game. A calm mind leads to consistent play and better results.

Actionable Insight: During practice matches this week practice responding calmly to frustrating situations. Bring yourself back to center by taking deep breaths before continuing play.

January 10
BUILD CONFIDENCE THROUGH ACTION

"Don't explain your philosophy. Embody it."

— Epictetus

Confidence isn't built through words or thoughts — it's built through consistent action and preparation. When you've put in the work during practice, you can trust yourself to perform well in matches. Confidence comes from knowing you've done everything possible to prepare for success, not from hoping for it. By focusing on what you do rather than what you say, you create a foundation of self-belief that lasts even in high-pressure situations. This habit of action over words strengthens both your skills and mindset over time.

Actionable Insight: Before your next match, reflect on all the preparation you've done leading up to it (e.g., hours spent practicing serves). Use this reflection as a source of confidence during play.

January 11
ADAPTABILITY IS STRENGTH

> "The wise man adapts himself to circumstances as water shapes itself to the vessel that contains it."
> — Seneca

Matches rarely go exactly as planned — your opponent might surprise you with unexpected tactics, or conditions like wind or heat might disrupt your rhythm. The ability to adapt quickly and effectively is what separates great players from good ones. Instead of resisting change, embrace it as part of the challenge and adjust your strategy accordingly. Adaptability requires staying calm under pressure and thinking creatively about solutions rather than dwelling on problems. By becoming more flexible, you make yourself harder to beat in any situation.

Actionable Insight: During practice this week, intentionally change variables (e.g., play on a different surface or use different tactics) and focus on staying adaptable.

January 12
LET GO OF PERFECTIONISM

> "Perfection is not attainable, but if we chase perfection we can catch excellence."
>
> – Vince Lombardi

Striving for perfection can lead to frustration because mistakes are inevitable in tennis. Instead of aiming for flawless play, focus on consistent improvement and learning from errors. Excellence comes from persistence and resilience rather than an unattainable ideal of perfection. By letting go of perfectionism, you free yourself from unnecessary pressure and allow yourself to play more naturally and confidently. Mistakes become opportunities for growth rather than sources of self-doubt.

Actionable Insight: During practice sessions this week, focus on effort rather than results (e.g., "Am I giving 100%?"). Celebrate progress instead of dwelling on mistakes.

January 13
DISCIPLINE OVER MOTIVATION

> "First say to yourself what you would be; and then do what you have to do."
>
> — Epictetus

Motivation comes and goes, but discipline is what keeps you moving forward even when motivation fades. Great players don't rely on fleeting feelings — they rely on habits and routines that ensure consistent effort over time. Discipline means showing up for practice even when you're tired or working on weaknesses that feel frustrating at first. By committing to disciplined action every day, you build momentum that leads to long-term success. This mindset helps you stay focused on your goals regardless of how you feel in the moment.

Actionable Insight: Create a daily tennis habit this week (e.g., practicing serves for 15 minutes). Stick to it no matter how motivated or unmotivated you feel.

January 14
FOCUS ON PROGRESS OVER TIME

> "Time is like a river made up of events which happen, and its current is strong; no sooner does anything appear than it is swept past and another comes in its place."
> — Marcus Aurelius

Improvement in tennis happens gradually over time — it's not about instant results but about consistent progress over weeks, months, and years. Rushing the process often leads to burnout or frustration because meaningful growth takes patience and persistence. By focusing on steady improvement rather than immediate outcomes, you stay motivated even when progress feels slow. Each small step forward contributes to long-term success if you trust the process and keep working hard. This mindset helps you appreciate how far you've come while staying committed to where you're going next.

 Actionable Insight: Reflect on one area where you've improved over the past month (e.g., footwork or consistency). Use this reflection as motivation to keep working toward your goals.

January 15
LEARN FROM EVERY LOSS

> "Difficulties strengthen the mind, as labor does the body."
> — Seneca

Losing a match isn't failure — it's feedback. Each loss reveals areas where you can improve, whether it's your strategy, technique, or mental game. Instead of dwelling on defeat, use it as an opportunity to grow stronger and prepare for future challenges. Losses are part of every player's journey, and those who embrace them as learning experiences ultimately become more resilient and adaptable. By reframing losses as lessons, you maintain a growth mindset that keeps you motivated to improve.

Actionable Insight: After your next match (win or lose), write down three things you did well and three areas where you can improve. Use this list to guide your next practice session.

January 16
STAY PRESENT IN EVERY POINT

"Confine yourself to the present."

— Marcus Aurelius

Thinking about past mistakes or worrying about the final score distracts you from playing your best tennis in the present moment. Staying fully focused on each point allows you to react instinctively and perform with clarity. By confining yourself to what's happening now, you reduce mental clutter and stay composed under pressure. Tennis is a game of moments, and success comes from winning one point at a time. The ability to reset after every point is one of the most valuable skills a player can develop.

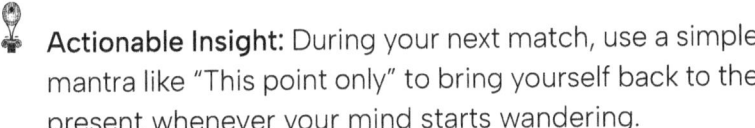 **Actionable Insight:** During your next match, use a simple mantra like "This point only" to bring yourself back to the present whenever your mind starts wandering.

January 17
RESILIENCE OVERCOMES FATIGUE

> "Endurance is one of the most difficult disciplines, but it is to the one who endures that the final victory comes."
> — SENECA

Long matches test not only your physical fitness but also your mental toughness. When fatigue sets in, resilience becomes the deciding factor — your ability to push through discomfort often determines the outcome. Resilience isn't just about enduring pain; it's about staying focused on your goals even when your body wants to quit. By training both your mind and body to handle fatigue, you gain an edge over opponents who falter under pressure. This discipline builds confidence in your ability to outlast challenges on and off the court.

Actionable Insight: During practice this week, simulate long matches by playing three full sets or running extra sprints at the end of your session. Focus on maintaining energy and focus even when tired.

January 18
HUMILITY IN VICTORY

> "Pride is a master of deception: when you think you're most free of it, you're most prone to it."
>
> — Seneca

Winning can sometimes lead to overconfidence or complacency, but true champions remain humble even after success. Humility allows you to recognize that there's always room for improvement and keeps you motivated to continue working hard. Arrogance after a win can lead to underestimating future opponents or neglecting areas that still need development. Staying grounded ensures that each victory becomes a stepping stone toward further growth rather than an endpoint. Humility also earns respect from others and strengthens your character as a competitor.

 Actionable Insight: After your next win, reflect on one area where your performance could have been better. Use this reflection as motivation for your next practice session.

January 19
EMBRACE DISCOMFORT

> "If you are distressed by anything external, the pain is not due to the thing itself but to your estimate of it; and this you have the power to revoke at any moment."
>
> — Marcus Aurelius

Improvement often requires stepping outside your comfort zone — whether it's pushing through tough drills or facing stronger opponents. Discomfort is temporary, but the growth it brings lasts forever. By reframing challenges as opportunities rather than threats, you build mental toughness and resilience that carry over into matches. Avoiding discomfort only limits your potential; embracing it helps you discover what you're truly capable of achieving. This mindset transforms difficult moments into valuable experiences for personal growth.

 Actionable Insight: Identify one area of discomfort in your training (e.g., practicing weaknesses or playing against tougher players) and commit to embracing it this week.

January 20
FOCUS ON WHAT YOU CAN IMPROVE

"Don't waste time arguing what a good man should be. Be one."

— Marcus Aurelius

It's easy to compare yourself to other players or dwell on what you lack, but true progress comes from focusing on what you can improve. Comparing yourself to others only distracts from your own journey and creates unnecessary frustration. Instead, channel that energy into identifying areas where you can grow and taking action to address them. Improvement isn't about being better than someone else — it's about being better than you were yesterday. This mindset keeps you motivated and focused on continuous self-improvement rather than external validation.

 Actionable Insight: Write down one specific aspect of your game (e.g., footwork) that needs improvement and create a plan for how you'll work on it during practice this week.

January 21
GRATITUDE FOR CHALLENGES

"The greater the difficulty, the more glory in surmounting it."
— Epictetus

Facing tough opponents or challenging conditions can feel overwhelming in the moment, but these are the matches that push you to grow. Challenges reveal weaknesses in your game and force you to adapt, making you a stronger and more well-rounded player. Instead of fearing difficult situations, embrace them as opportunities to test your resilience and improve. Gratitude for challenges shifts your mindset from frustration to determination, helping you rise to the occasion. Over time, these experiences become the foundation of your success.

Actionable Insight: After your next tough match or practice session, write down one way it helped you improve as a player. Reflect on how challenges have shaped your growth.

January 22
THE VALUE OF CONSISTENCY

"No man is free who is not master of himself."

— Epictetus

Freedom on the tennis court — and in life — comes from self-mastery. The Stoics believed that true autonomy is achieved by disciplining your impulses and emotions, not by indulging them. In tennis, this means sticking to your routines, maintaining focus under pressure, and holding yourself accountable for your actions. Self-mastery allows you to play with clarity and purpose, regardless of external distractions.

 Actionable Insight: Identify one impulse that undermines your tennis (e.g., reacting to mistakes, losing focus). For the next week, practice noticing and redirecting this impulse every time it appears.

January 23
STAY CALM UNDER PRESSURE

> "If you are pained by external things, it is not they that disturb you, but your own judgment of them. And it is in your power to wipe out that judgment now."
>
> — Marcus Aurelius

Pressure situations — like break points or tiebreakers — can feel overwhelming if you let fear or doubt take over. However, pressure is only as powerful as you allow it to be; it's your perception of the situation that creates stress. By reframing pressure as an opportunity rather than a threat, you can stay calm and focused on executing your game plan. A composed mind allows you to think clearly and perform at your best when it matters most. Mastering this skill gives you an edge over opponents who crumble under pressure.

Actionable Insight: During practice matches this week, simulate high-pressure situations (e.g., playing tiebreakers). Focus on controlling your breathing and staying present in each point.

January 24
LEARN FROM MISTAKES WITHOUT SELF-BLAME

"To err is human; to persist in error is diabolical."
— Seneca

Mistakes are inevitable in tennis — every player misses shots or makes poor decisions during matches. The key is not to dwell on these errors but to learn from them without falling into self-blame or frustration. Analyzing mistakes objectively allows you to make adjustments and improve without damaging your confidence. By viewing errors as part of the learning process rather than personal failures, you maintain a positive mindset that supports growth. This approach helps you bounce back quickly and stay focused on the next point.

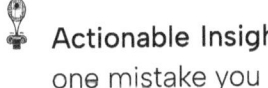 **Actionable Insight:** After each match this week, review one mistake you made and identify what caused it (e.g., poor footwork or hesitation). Use this insight to guide your next practice session.

January 25
BUILD CONFIDENCE THROUGH PREPARATION

> "Confidence is not 'They will like me.' Confidence is 'I'll be fine if they don't.'"
>
> – MARCUS AURELIUS

True confidence doesn't come from external validation — it comes from knowing you've done everything possible to prepare for success. When you've put in the work during practice, you can trust yourself to perform well regardless of external factors like tough opponents or critical spectators. Preparation builds a foundation of self-belief that remains steady even in high-pressure situations. By focusing on what's within your control — your effort and preparation — you free yourself from worrying about others' opinions or outcomes beyond your influence. This internal confidence makes you a stronger competitor on court.

Actionable Insight: Before your next match, spend time reflecting on all the preparation you've done leading up to it (e.g., drills, fitness training). Use this reflection as a source of confidence during play.

January 26
FIND JOY IN COMPETITION

> "The happiness of your life depends upon the quality of your thoughts."
>
> — MARCUS AURELIUS

It's easy to get caught up in results — winning or losing — but true joy comes from embracing the competition itself. Every match is an opportunity to test yourself against an opponent, push your limits, and experience the thrill of battle. By focusing on the process rather than the outcome, you can find fulfillment in every point played. A positive mindset transforms competition into a rewarding experience rather than a source of stress or frustration. This perspective helps you stay motivated and enjoy the game regardless of results.

 Actionable Insight: During your next match, focus on enjoying each rally and appreciating the challenge of competing against your opponent.

January 27
TRUST YOUR TRAINING

> "It is not things themselves that disturb us, but our opinions about them."
>
> – Epictetus

Your experience on the court is shaped not by events, but by your interpretation of them. A missed shot is just a shot; it's your opinion — frustration, disappointment, or self-criticism — that turns it into a setback. The Stoics remind us that we have the power to choose our perspective. By adopting a mindset of learning and resilience, you turn every moment, good or bad, into fuel for growth.

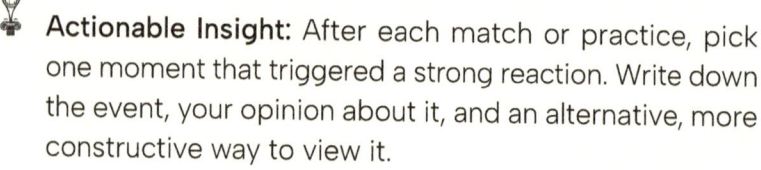 **Actionable Insight:** After each match or practice, pick one moment that triggered a strong reaction. Write down the event, your opinion about it, and an alternative, more constructive way to view it.

January 28
GRATITUDE FOR TENNIS

> "Take full account of what excellences you possess, and in gratitude remember how you would hanker after them if you had them not."
>
> — Marcus Aurelius

It's easy to get caught up in frustrations — missed shots, tough losses, or slow progress — but don't forget how fortunate you are to play the game at all. Tennis gives you the chance to challenge yourself, grow stronger, and experience moments of joy and competition. Gratitude shifts your focus from what's lacking to what's fulfilling about the game. By appreciating tennis as a gift rather than a burden, you cultivate a positive mindset that fuels motivation and enjoyment. This gratitude helps you stay connected to why you love the sport in the first place.

Actionable Insight: Before your next practice or match, take a moment to reflect on what tennis has brought into your life — whether it's friendships, fitness, or personal growth.

January 29
PATIENCE WITH PROGRESS

> "How ridiculous and how strange to be surprised at anything which happens in life!"
>
> — Marcus Aurelius

Improvement in tennis is rarely linear — it's natural to have setbacks or plateaus along the way. Expecting instant results only leads to frustration; instead, trust that consistent effort over time will yield progress. Patience allows you to embrace the ups and downs of training without losing sight of your long-term goals. By accepting that growth takes time, you free yourself from unnecessary stress and focus on steady improvement. This mindset helps you stay motivated even when progress feels slow.

Actionable Insight: Reflect on one area where your game has improved over the past six months (e.g., consistency or fitness). Use this reflection as a reminder that progress happens gradually.

January 30
FINISH STRONG

> "The last part of life is like the end of a play — only the actors know how it turns out."
>
> — SENECA

Many matches are won or lost in their final moments when fatigue sets in and mental focus wavers. Staying strong until the very end requires discipline and determination — you can't let up just because victory seems close or defeat feels inevitable. The ability to finish strong separates great players from average ones, as it demonstrates resilience and focus under pressure. By treating every point as equally important, especially near the end of a match, you give yourself the best chance to succeed. This approach ensures that no matter the outcome, you've given your all until the final shot.

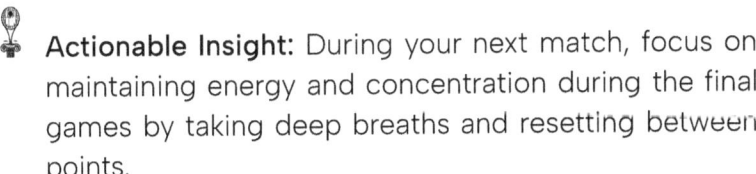 **Actionable Insight:** During your next match, focus on maintaining energy and concentration during the final games by taking deep breaths and resetting between points.

January 31
REFLECT ON YOUR GROWTH

> "When we are no longer able to change a situation, we are challenged to change ourselves."
>
> — Viktor Frankl
> (inspired by Stoic themes)

Reflection is an essential part of growth — taking time to evaluate how far you've come helps you identify strengths and areas for improvement. Tennis constantly challenges you to adapt and evolve both physically and mentally. By reflecting on your experiences over the past month — your wins, losses, and lessons — you can set clear goals for continued growth. This process fosters self-awareness and keeps you motivated for what lies ahead. Reflection isn't about dwelling on mistakes but learning from them and celebrating progress.

 Actionable Insight: Write down three things you've learned about yourself as a player this month and one specific goal for February.

January Wrap-Up

With January complete, we've laid the foundation for mental toughness through lessons on controlling emotions, embracing challenges, staying patient with progress, and reflecting on growth. Each day builds resilience both on and off the court.

February

Passions and Emotions – Mastering Your Inner World

FEBRUARY FOCUSES ON understanding and mastering your emotions — the true battleground for every competitor. While passion fuels your drive, unchecked emotions can cloud judgment and disrupt performance. This month, you'll learn to recognize impulses, respond rather than react, and channel your energy constructively. By applying Stoic principles, you'll gain greater self-control, resilience, and clarity, turning emotions into an asset both on and off the court.

February 1
UNDERSTANDING OUR IMPULSES

> "Frame your thoughts like this — you are an old person, you won't let yourself be enslaved by this any longer, no longer pulled like a puppet by every impulse, and you'll stop complaining about your present fortune or dreading the future."
>
> — Marcus Aurelius

In tennis, impulses can lead to rash decisions on the court, such as going for an ill-advised winner or letting frustration affect your play. By imagining yourself as a wise, experienced player, you can better control these impulses and make more strategic choices. This mindset helps you avoid complaining about bad calls or worrying about the match outcome, keeping you focused on the present point. Mastering your impulses allows you to play with a clear mind, making decisions based on strategy rather than emotion. Over time, this control over your impulses becomes a powerful tool, helping you maintain composure in high-pressure situations and play more consistently.

Actionable Insight: Before your next match, take a moment to visualize yourself as a seasoned, composed player. Use this image to guide your decisions and reactions during play.

February 2
BALANCING PASSION AND REASON

> "To wish to be well is a part of becoming well."
> — Seneca

Passion for tennis is crucial, driving you to practice and compete with intensity. However, this passion must be balanced with reason to avoid burnout or reckless play. Wishing to improve is the first step, but it must be followed by thoughtful, consistent action. This balance allows you to channel your enthusiasm productively while maintaining a clear perspective on your development. By combining your love for the game with rational training methods and match strategies, you create a sustainable approach to improvement. Remember, the most successful players are those who can harness their passion within the framework of disciplined, reasoned practice and play.

Actionable Insight: Write down one passionate goal you have for your tennis game, then create a rational, step-by-step plan to achieve it. Ensure your plan includes both technical practice and mental preparation.

February 3
EMBRACING DISCOMFORT

> "If you accomplish something good with hard work, the labor passes quickly, but the good endures; if you do something shameful in pursuit of pleasure, the pleasure passes quickly, but the shame endures."
>
> — MUSONIUS RUFUS

In tennis, growth often comes through embracing discomfort, whether it's grueling practice sessions or challenging matches against superior opponents. The temporary discomfort of hard work leads to lasting improvements in your game. Conversely, avoiding difficult training or competitive situations might feel good in the moment but can hinder your long-term progress. By embracing the challenges and discomfort that come with serious training, you build not only physical skills but also mental resilience. This willingness to endure short-term difficulties for long-term gains is what separates great players from those who plateau.

 Actionable Insight: This week, intentionally incorporate one challenging drill or practice routine that pushes you out of your comfort zone. Reflect on how overcoming this discomfort contributes to your growth as a player.

February 4
MANAGING EXPECTATIONS

> "When we are no longer able to change a situation, we are challenged to change ourselves."
> — Viktor Frankl
> (inspired by Stoic philosophy)

In tennis, as in life, we often face situations beyond our control — an opponent's skill level, weather conditions, or even our own physical limitations on a given day. The key to success lies not in trying to control these external factors, but in managing our expectations and responses to them. By focusing on what you can control — your effort, attitude, and strategy — rather than external outcomes, you free yourself from unnecessary frustration. This shift in perspective allows you to adapt more readily to challenging situations and maintain focus on your performance. Remember, true mastery in tennis comes not from always winning, but from consistently giving your best effort regardless of circumstances.

Actionable Insight: Before your next match, set goals based on factors within your control (e.g., maintaining a positive attitude, executing your game plan) rather than outcome-based goals.

February 5
THE POWER OF PRESENT FOCUS

> "True happiness is... to enjoy the present, without anxious dependence upon the future."
>
> — SENECA

In tennis, it's easy to get caught up worrying about the outcome of a match or fixating on past mistakes. However, true performance excellence comes from immersing yourself fully in the present moment. By focusing on the current point, rather than the potential final score, you free yourself to play without the burden of anxiety or regret. This present-focused mindset allows for quicker reactions, clearer decision-making, and a more enjoyable playing experience. Moreover, by stringing together a series of well-played present moments, you naturally increase your chances of achieving the desired outcome without the added pressure of constantly thinking about it.

Actionable Insight: In your next match, practice resetting your focus to the present moment between each point. Use a physical cue, like touching your strings, to trigger this mental reset.

February 6
RESPOND, DON'T REACT

> "It is best to reject straight away the first inducements to anger, to resist it from the very beginning."
>
> — SENECA

Tennis is a game of constant emotional tests. A bad line call, an opponent's lucky net cord, or your own unforced error can trigger a surge of anger or frustration. The Stoics teach us that the first spark of anger is the most dangerous — if you let it catch, it can quickly become a wildfire, consuming your focus and ruining your match. Instead, practice catching that first impulse. When you feel irritation rising after a setback, pause and breathe. Remind yourself that the situation itself is neutral; it's your reaction that gives it power. By learning to respond with calm deliberation rather than reacting impulsively, you protect your mental state and keep your attention on the next point. Over time, this habit builds emotional resilience, allowing you to remain steady and composed no matter what the match throws at you.

 Actionable Insight: In your next match, make a conscious effort to notice the very first signs of frustration or anger. When they arise, take a deep breath and count to three before acting. Use this pause to reset your focus and choose a response that serves your game, not your emotions.

February 7
ACCEPTING CHANGE AND UNCERTAINTY

> "Everywhere there is change, yet we need to fear nothing."
> – Marcus Aurelius

Change is a constant in tennis. The weather can shift from sunny to windy in a matter of minutes, the bounce of the ball can be unpredictable, and your opponent might suddenly switch tactics. Many players waste energy resisting these changes, wishing conditions were different or that their opponent would play a certain way. The Stoic approach is to accept change as an inevitable part of the game and to meet it with equanimity. When you stop fearing or resenting change, you free up mental energy to adapt and respond creatively. This adaptability becomes a competitive advantage, allowing you to thrive in dynamic situations and to see every new challenge as an opportunity to grow.

Actionable Insight: Before your next practice or match, remind yourself that change is not an enemy but an essential part of tennis. When something unexpected happens, repeat to yourself: "This is part of the game. I accept it and adapt."

February 8
THE VALUE OF SELF-DISCIPLINE

> "Nothing is good unless it helps you to become just, self-disciplined, courageous, and independent. Nothing is bad, except what does the opposite."
>
> – Marcus Aurelius

Self-discipline is the backbone of progress in tennis. It's what gets you on the court for early morning practices, keeps you working on your weaknesses, and helps you stick to your game plan under pressure. The Stoics believed that true good comes from developing virtues like self-discipline, not from fleeting pleasures or easy victories. In tennis, this means prioritizing long-term growth over short-term gratification. It's easy to skip the tough drills or give up when you're tired, but every act of discipline strengthens your resolve and builds the habits that lead to excellence. Over time, these small acts of discipline compound, transforming your game and your character.

Actionable Insight: Identify one area of your tennis routine that requires more discipline — whether it's fitness, nutrition, or mental training. Set a specific, measurable goal for the week (e.g., "I will practice my second serve for 20 minutes every day") and hold yourself accountable.

February 9
LET GO OF JUDGMENTS

> "Forget how you look to others. Be content to live the rest of your life as decided by nature."
>
> — Marcus Aurelius

Many players are distracted by how they appear to others — whether it's worrying about looking foolish after a missed shot or being judged for losing to a lower-ranked opponent. This external focus creates anxiety and pulls you away from your best tennis. The Stoics remind us that our value doesn't come from others' opinions, but from living in accordance with our own principles and nature. On the court, this means playing for your own growth and enjoyment, not for the approval or admiration of spectators or opponents. When you let go of the need to impress, you free yourself to play more authentically and courageously.

Actionable Insight: In your next match, whenever you notice yourself worrying about what others think, bring your focus back to your own process. Repeat the mantra: "I play for my own growth, not for their approval."

February 10
THE POWER OF REASON OVER PASSION

> "Passion and reason, as I said before, don't have distinct provinces. Rather the mind itself changes for better or for worse."
>
> — SENECA

Passion for tennis is a double-edged sword — it can fuel your motivation, but if unchecked, it can also lead to rash decisions and emotional outbursts. The Stoics teach that reason and passion are not separate forces; rather, your mind can be guided by either, depending on your habits and choices. On the court, this means using your passion to energize your play, but always letting reason steer your decisions. When you feel your emotions rising — whether it's excitement, frustration, or anxiety — pause and ask yourself: "What's the smartest play right now?" Over time, training your mind to default to reason in the heat of competition will make you a more consistent and formidable player.

 Actionable Insight: During your next practice, pay attention to moments when your emotions threaten to take over. Practice pausing, taking a breath, and making a deliberate, reasoned choice about your next shot or tactic.

February 11
DETACHMENT FROM OUTCOMES

> "Soon you will be dead and forgotten. Meanwhile, if what you do is fit for a rational and social being, why worry about anything else?"
>
> – Marcus Aurelius

The pressure to win can be overwhelming, leading to anxiety and tightness on court. The Stoics remind us of the fleeting nature of all things, including our tennis achievements and failures. In the grand scheme, the outcome of today's match will soon be forgotten by everyone — including yourself. What endures is how you conducted yourself: Did you play with integrity, effort, and respect? By focusing on what is "fit for a rational and social being" — your effort, your sportsmanship, your process — you free yourself from the burden of results. This detachment paradoxically allows you to play more freely and often leads to better outcomes.

Actionable Insight: Before your next match, set an intention to focus on your effort and attitude, not the result. After the match, reflect only on what you could control, letting go of the final score.

February 12
THE DANGERS OF ANGER

> "Anger sometimes overthrows and breaks to pieces whatever it meets. Yet more often it causes its own destruction."
>
> — SENECA

Anger on the tennis court is like a double fault — it not only sabotages your current point, but it can unravel your entire match. While it's natural to feel upset after a bad call or a missed opportunity, giving in to anger almost always makes things worse. The Stoics warn that anger is self-destructive; it clouds your judgment, tightens your muscles, and distracts you from the task at hand. The best players learn to acknowledge their anger without letting it dictate their actions. They use it as a signal to refocus, not as fuel for negative behavior. By mastering your anger, you protect your performance and your reputation.

 Actionable Insight: When you feel anger rising during a match, use it as a cue to slow down. Take a few deep breaths, walk to the back fence, and remind yourself: "Anger helps no one — not me, not my game."

February 13
THE FREEDOM OF ACCEPTANCE

> "There is only one way to be happy. Keep this thought ready for use morning, noon, and night. Give up the desire for things not under your control. Don't think of anything as your own."
>
> — EPICTETUS

Much of the frustration in tennis comes from wanting things to go a certain way — wanting the weather to be perfect, your opponent to make errors, or the umpire to always rule in your favor. The Stoics teach that happiness comes from releasing your grip on these uncontrollable desires. On the court, this means accepting every situation as it comes and focusing only on your own actions and responses. When you stop demanding that things go your way, you experience a sense of freedom and lightness, which allows you to play your best tennis. Acceptance is not resignation; it's the foundation for focused, joyful performance.

Actionable Insight: Before your next match, make a list of things you cannot control (e.g., weather, opponent's play, line calls). Consciously release your attachment to these, and commit to focusing only on your effort and attitude.

February 14
THE IMPORTANCE OF COURTESY AND RESPECT

> "Fix your eyes on what you have to do. Remember, you must be a good human being. Do what nature demands of you without hesitation. Speak what is just as you see it, but do so with courtesy, modesty, and sincerity."
> — Marcus Aurelius

Tennis is as much a test of character as it is of skill. How you treat your opponent, the officials, and even yourself in moments of stress reveals your true nature. The Stoics believed that virtue is the highest good, and that courtesy, modesty, and sincerity are essential parts of a virtuous life. On the court, this means making honest line calls, congratulating your opponent on good shots, and accepting losses with grace. By making respect and courtesy your default, you not only honor the spirit of the game but also build a reputation as a player others admire and want to emulate.

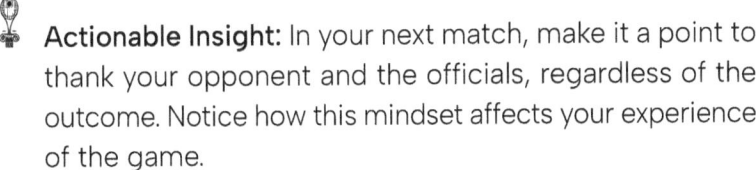

Actionable Insight: In your next match, make it a point to thank your opponent and the officials, regardless of the outcome. Notice how this mindset affects your experience of the game.

February 15
THE WISDOM OF LETTING GO

> "It is the proper time. Let go of all your dislikes. Why are you like a donkey enduring the burden?"
>
> — Epictetus

Holding onto grudges — against opponents, officials, or even yourself — only weighs you down and saps your energy. The Stoics urge us to let go of dislikes and resentments, recognizing that they serve no constructive purpose. In tennis, this might mean forgiving yourself for a double fault, moving on from a disputed call, or letting go of frustration with an opponent's playing style. The lighter you travel emotionally, the more freely and creatively you can play. Letting go is not about ignoring problems, but about refusing to be burdened by what you cannot change.

 Actionable Insight: After your next match, reflect on any lingering frustrations or resentments. Write them down, acknowledge them, and then consciously let them go. Notice how this emotional release improves your mindset for future matches.

February 16
THE POWER OF PERCEPTION

> "Wealth consists not in having great possessions, but in having few wants."
>
> — Epictetus

In tennis, real strength doesn't come from fancy gear, accolades, or a perfect match record — it comes from simplicity. When you reduce your mental clutter and narrow your focus to what really matters — effort, improvement, and joy for the game — you become mentally free and more grounded under pressure. The less you *need* the game to give you something, the more you'll get out of it.

Actionable Insight: Before your next match, set one simple intention (e.g., "Compete fully each point") and repeat it between games. Let go of extra expectations and play with presence.

February 17
ENDURE WITHOUT COMPLAINT

> "If it is endurable, then endure it. Stop complaining."
> – Marcus Aurelius

Tennis is a test of endurance — not just physically, but mentally and emotionally. You will face fatigue, pain, and adversity, especially in long matches or tough training blocks. The Stoic approach is to accept what you can endure and to do so without complaint. Complaining drains your energy and shifts your focus away from solutions. By quietly enduring discomfort, you build inner strength and resilience. This mindset allows you to push through tough moments, outlast your opponent, and finish strong. Endurance is not just about surviving hardship, but about embracing it as a necessary part of the journey toward mastery.

Actionable Insight: During your next grueling practice or match, make a conscious effort not to complain — internally or externally. When you feel discomfort, repeat the phrase: "If it is endurable, then endure it." Channel your energy into your performance, not your complaints.

February 18
THE BEST REVENGE

> "The best revenge is not to be like your enemy."
> — Marcus Aurelius

In the heat of competition, it's easy to be tempted to stoop to your opponent's level — whether that means arguing calls, showing poor sportsmanship, or playing mind games. The Stoics remind us that the highest form of "revenge" is to remain true to your own values, regardless of how others behave. In tennis, this means maintaining your integrity, composure, and respect for the game, even when provoked. By refusing to mirror negative behavior, you protect your own character and set a standard for others. This inner discipline not only earns you respect but also keeps your mind clear and focused on what matters: playing your best tennis.

 Actionable Insight: If your opponent acts disrespectfully or tries to rattle you, take a deep breath and remind yourself: "I will not be like my enemy." Respond with calm and fairness, letting your actions speak for your character.

February 19
THE WISDOM OF SELF-REFLECTION

> "I will keep constant watch over myself and — most usefully — will put each day up for review. For this is what makes us evil — that none of us looks back upon our own lives."
> — SENECA

Improvement in tennis requires honest self-reflection. It's not enough to simply play matches and attend practices — you must also review your actions, decisions, and attitudes. The Stoics believed that daily self-examination is essential for growth. After each session, ask yourself: Did I stay focused? Did I manage my emotions? Did I give my best effort? By regularly putting your day "up for review," you identify strengths to build on and weaknesses to address. This habit fosters continuous improvement and prevents you from repeating the same mistakes.

Actionable Insight: After every practice or match this week, spend five minutes journaling: What did I do well today? Where can I improve? Use these insights to set specific goals for your next session.

February 20
THE FREEDOM OF CLARITY

> "Wisdom — even a tiny bit — is clarity. Clarity is freedom."
> — EPICTETUS

of mind is one of the greatest assets a tennis player can possess. When your thoughts are muddled by anxiety, doubt, or distraction, your performance suffers. The Stoics teach that wisdom brings clarity, and clarity brings freedom — from fear, from indecision, from self-imposed limitations. In tennis, this means knowing your game plan, understanding your strengths and weaknesses, and seeing each situation for what it is. When you approach the court with a clear mind, you are free to play instinctively and creatively, unburdened by confusion or hesitation.

 Actionable Insight: Before your next match, take a few moments to clarify your intentions: What is my strategy? What are my goals for today? Return to this clarity whenever you feel yourself drifting into doubt or distraction.

February 21
CHOOSE NOT TO BE HARMED

> "Choose not to be harmed — and you won't feel harmed. Don't feel harmed — and you haven't been."
> — MARCUS AURELIUS

In tennis, perceived slights — like a questionable call, an opponent's celebration, or a coach's criticism — can feel deeply personal. But the Stoics remind us that harm is a choice: you are only harmed if you allow yourself to feel harmed. By choosing not to take things personally, you protect your confidence and focus. This doesn't mean ignoring feedback or refusing to learn from mistakes; it means refusing to let external events dictate your self-worth or emotional state. The power to remain unshaken lies within you.

Actionable Insight: The next time you feel slighted or wronged on court, pause and ask yourself: "Am I truly harmed, or am I choosing to feel harmed?" Practice letting go of perceived insults and returning your focus to the game.

February 22
THE DISCIPLINE OF SAYING NO

> "It may take some hard work. But the more you say no to the things that don't matter, the more you can say yes to the things that do."
>
> — The Daily Stoic

Discipline in tennis isn't just about training hard — it's also about making wise choices with your time and energy. Every "yes" to a distraction is a "no" to your goals. The Stoics advocate for a life of focus and intention, paring away what is unnecessary so you can give your best to what truly matters. This means saying no to late nights, unhealthy habits, or negative self-talk, and saying yes to rest, recovery, and purposeful practice. The discipline to prioritize your values over your impulses is what separates the dedicated from the distracted.

Actionable Insight: Identify one habit or activity that is not serving your tennis goals. Commit to saying "no" to it this week, and use that time or energy to reinforce a positive habit instead.

February 23
THE PRESENT MOMENT IS ALL YOU HAVE

> "Were you to live three thousand years, or even a countless multiple of that, keep in mind that no one ever loses a life other than the one they are living… The present moment lasts the same for all and is all anyone possesses."
> — Marcus Aurelius

Tennis is a game played in the present. The past — missed shots, lost sets — or the future — what if I lose? — can distract you from the only thing you truly have: this point, right now. The Stoics urge us to remember that the present moment is all we ever possess. By anchoring yourself in the now, you perform with greater freedom, awareness, and joy. This mindset not only improves your game but also enriches your experience of the sport.

  Actionable Insight: During your next match, use a physical cue (like bouncing the ball before your serve) to bring your attention back to the present. Whenever you catch your mind wandering, gently return to the current point.

February 24
BE TOLERANT WITH OTHERS, STRICT WITH YOURSELF

"Be tolerant with others and strict with yourself."
— Marcus Aurelius

It's easy to judge others harshly for their mistakes while excusing your own lapses. The Stoic way is the opposite: hold yourself to the highest standards, but extend patience and understanding to those around you. In tennis, this means being honest about your own effort, focus, and attitude, while showing empathy toward your opponent, your doubles partner, or the officials. This approach fosters humility and self-improvement while building stronger relationships on and off the court.

Actionable Insight: After your next match, reflect honestly on your own performance and attitude. If you catch yourself criticizing others, pause and redirect that energy toward your own growth and self-discipline.

February 25
KNOWLEDGE IS FREEDOM

> "Knowledge — self-knowledge in particular — is freedom."
> – THE DAILY STOIC

Understanding yourself — your strengths, weaknesses, triggers, and tendencies — is the foundation of both Stoic philosophy and tennis excellence. The more you know about your own game and mindset, the more freedom you have to make wise choices under pressure. Self-knowledge allows you to prepare better, adapt faster, and recover from setbacks with resilience. In tennis, this means being honest about what works for you, what needs improvement, and how you respond to adversity.

Actionable Insight: This week, take time after each practice to honestly assess your performance: What did I do well? Where did I struggle? Use this self-knowledge to set targeted goals for your next session.

February 26
THE VALUE OF PREPARATION

> "The more we value things outside our control, the less control we have."
>
> — EPICTETUS

In tennis, it's tempting to focus on the conditions, the draw, or even the "luck" of the net cord. But real progress comes from investing your energy in what you can control: your preparation, your attitude, and your effort. The more you obsess over external factors, the more powerless you feel. The Stoics remind us that true power is found in mastering your own actions and mindset. By letting go of the need to control outcomes, you free yourself to prepare thoroughly and perform with confidence, regardless of circumstances.

Actionable Insight: Before your next match, write down three things you can control and three you cannot. During play, check in with yourself and redirect your focus to your preparation and effort whenever your mind drifts to external factors.

February 27
THE ART OF LISTENING

> "We have two ears and one mouth, so that we can listen twice as much as we speak."
>
> — Epictetus

Tennis players often focus on expressing themselves — through their play, their strategy, their emotions. But the Stoics valued listening as a path to wisdom. On the court, listening means paying close attention: to your coach's advice, your opponent's patterns, and your own body's signals. It means being open to feedback and willing to learn from every situation. By listening more than you speak or act, you gather valuable information that can give you an edge. The best players are students of the game, always attuned to what is happening around them and within them.

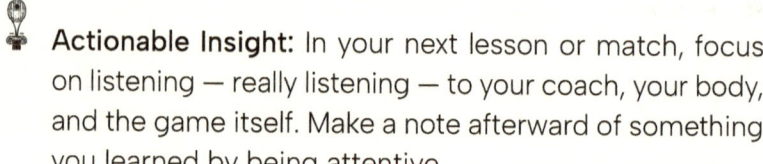

Actionable Insight: In your next lesson or match, focus on listening — really listening — to your coach, your body, and the game itself. Make a note afterward of something you learned by being attentive.

February 28
CONTROL YOUR DESIRES

"Freedom is not achieved by satisfying desire, but by eliminating it."

— Epictetus

Desire can be a powerful motivator, but unchecked, it leads to frustration and disappointment. The Stoics teach that true freedom comes not from getting everything you want, but from mastering your desires. In tennis, this means letting go of the craving for easy wins, perfect conditions, or constant praise. Instead, focus on the process — on effort, learning, and growth. When you are no longer attached to specific outcomes, you play with greater freedom, joy, and resilience.

 Actionable Insight: Before your next match, notice any desires or expectations you're holding onto. Practice letting them go, and commit to playing for the love of the game itself.

February 29
THE PRESENT IS YOUR KINGDOM

> "He who lives in harmony with himself lives in harmony with the universe."
>
> — MARCUS AURELIUS

Harmony on the court comes from being fully present — accepting yourself, your abilities, and your circumstances in this moment. When you are at peace with yourself, you are less likely to be thrown off by adversity or distracted by external pressures. The Stoics saw living in the present as the key to tranquility. In tennis, this means focusing on the point at hand, embracing both your strengths and weaknesses, and playing with authenticity. When you are in harmony with yourself, your game flows naturally, and you experience the deep satisfaction that comes from giving your best.

 Actionable Insight: At the start of your next session, take a few deep breaths and remind yourself: "This is my court, this is my moment." Play each point as if it is the only one that matters.

February Wrap-Up

As February ends, you've learned to recognize, manage, and channel your emotions on and off the court. By mastering your inner world, you've built greater self-control, clarity, and resilience — skills that will serve you in every match and every challenge ahead.

March Introduction

The Obstacle Is the Way – Turning Adversity Into Advantage

MARCH IS ABOUT embracing adversity as your greatest teacher. This month, you'll discover how setbacks, tough opponents, and unexpected challenges can become stepping stones to growth. By applying Stoic wisdom, you'll learn to turn every obstacle into an opportunity, building strength and confidence with each test you face.

March 1
THE OBSTACLE BECOMES THE PATH

> "Difficulties show men what they are."
>
> — Epictetus

Every tough match, every setback, and every challenge on court is a mirror, reflecting your true character. The Stoics believed that adversity is the ultimate test of who we are. In tennis, how you respond when things get tough — whether you fight, adapt, or give up — reveals your inner strength. Instead of resenting obstacles, see them as opportunities to demonstrate resilience and to discover what you're truly capable of.

 Actionable Insight: After your next challenging match, reflect on how you responded to adversity. Identify one way you can strengthen your response for the future.

March 2
PERSIST AND PREVAIL

"To bear trials with a calm mind robs misfortune of its strength and burden."

— Seneca

A calm mind is your greatest ally in difficult moments. The Stoics teach that how you bear adversity determines its impact on you. On the court, the player who remains composed in the face of setbacks is less likely to be overwhelmed by them. Calmness allows you to think clearly, adapt, and keep fighting, no matter the score.

 Actionable Insight: Practice a calming ritual — such as deep breathing or a short mantra — whenever you face a setback in practice or a match. Notice how this helps you regain control and composure.

March 3
ADAPT AND OVERCOME

> "Don't hope that events will turn out the way you want, welcome events in whichever way they happen: this is the path to peace."
>
> — Epictetus

Tennis rarely goes exactly as planned. Your opponent might play better than expected, your serve might desert you, or rain might interrupt your rhythm. The Stoics teach that peace comes from accepting reality as it is, not as you wish it to be. On the court, this means adapting your tactics, staying flexible, and welcoming the unexpected as a chance to learn and grow. The more you practice acceptance and adaptability, the more resilient and resourceful you become.

 Actionable Insight: In your next match, when something doesn't go your way, pause and say to yourself: "I welcome this. I will adapt." Notice how this attitude affects your performance.

March 4
STRENGTH THROUGH ADVERSITY

> "No man is more unhappy than he who never faces adversity. For he is not permitted to prove himself."
> — SENECA

Adversity is the proving ground for both the mind and the spirit. The Stoics remind us that a life — or a tennis career — without challenge is one without the chance to discover your true potential. On court, the difficult matches and moments when you want to give up are not punishments, but opportunities to demonstrate your resilience and to grow stronger. Each struggle is a chance to prove to yourself what you're capable of, and to emerge wiser and more prepared for whatever comes next.

Actionable Insight: After your next tough match or practice, write down one way the challenge allowed you to prove something to yourself. Reflect on how this adversity is shaping you into a more resilient competitor.

March 5
TURN SETBACKS INTO STRENGTH

> "Fire is the test of gold; adversity, of strong men."
> — SENECA

Setbacks are inevitable in tennis — injuries, losses, or periods of poor form. The Stoics believed that adversity is the true measure of character. Just as gold is tested by fire, you are tested by your response to setbacks. Will you let them defeat you, or will you use them to refine your resolve and commitment? Every setback contains the seed of growth if you approach it with the right mindset.

Actionable Insight: Think of a recent setback in your tennis journey. How can you use it to become stronger, wiser, or more determined? Make a plan to turn this adversity into an advantage.

March 6
FOCUS ON WHAT YOU CAN CONTROL

"Some things are up to us and some things are not."
— Epictetus

In tennis, as in life, much is outside your control: the weather, your opponent's skill, the surface, even the crowd. The Stoics teach that peace and effectiveness come from focusing only on what you can control — your effort, your attitude, your preparation. By letting go of everything else, you conserve your energy for what truly matters and avoid needless frustration. This mindset not only improves your performance but also brings a sense of calm and confidence, no matter the circumstances.

 Actionable Insight: Before your next match, make a list of what is within your control and what is not. Commit to focusing only on the former, and practice letting go of the rest.

March 7
EMBRACE DISCOMFORT

> "Smooth seas do not make skillful sailors."
> — AFRICAN PROVERB
> (STOIC-ADJACENT)

It's easy to play well when everything goes your way, but true growth happens when you're tested by difficult conditions, tough opponents, or your own doubts. The Stoics remind us that discomfort is the training ground for skill and resilience. In tennis, seek out those "rough seas" — the tough drills, the long matches, the moments when you want to quit. These are the experiences that shape you into a skillful, adaptable, and courageous competitor.

 Actionable Insight: Choose one area of your tennis game that makes you uncomfortable. This week, lean into it and track how facing it head-on builds your confidence and skill.

March 8
LEARN FROM EVERY OPPONENT

"From every event, try to extract what is useful."
— Epictetus

Every opponent, whether stronger or weaker, has something to teach you. The Stoics encourage us to approach every situation as a learning opportunity. In tennis, this means analyzing your matches not just for wins and losses, but for insights — about your technique, your mindset, your tactics. Even a loss can be a victory if you extract a lesson from it. This attitude transforms every match into a stepping stone on your journey of improvement.

Actionable Insight: After your next match, regardless of the outcome, write down three things you learned — about yourself, your game, or your opponent.

March 9
PATIENCE IN PROGRESS

> "Patience is the companion of wisdom."
> — AUGUSTINE OF HIPPO
> (STOIC-ADJACENT)

Progress in tennis is rarely quick or linear. The Stoics valued patience as a sign of wisdom, knowing that lasting improvement comes from steady, persistent effort. When you're frustrated by slow gains or setbacks, remember that patience allows you to keep learning, growing, and enjoying the process. Each practice, each match, each small step forward is a building block for future success.

Actionable Insight: Set a long-term tennis goal and break it into small, achievable steps. Celebrate each bit of progress, and remind yourself that patience is a key part of your journey.

March 10
REFRAME FAILURE AS FEEDBACK

> "A setback has often cleared the way for greater prosperity. Many things have fallen only to rise to more exalted heights."
> — SENECA

Failure is not the end, but a necessary part of the path to success. The Stoics teach that setbacks are often the prelude to greater achievements. In tennis, every loss, every mistake, every disappointment is feedback — a chance to learn, adapt, and come back stronger. By reframing failure as a stepping stone rather than a stumbling block, you build resilience and open yourself to greater possibilities.

Actionable Insight: After your next loss, spend time reflecting on what it can teach you. Write down one concrete adjustment you can make as a result of this experience, and commit to applying it in your next match.

March 11
YOUR REACTION IS YOUR POWER

> "It's not what happens to you, but how you react to it that matters."
>
> – Epictetus

On the court, you cannot control every bounce, call, or opponent's move. But you always control your reaction. The Stoics teach that our responses shape our reality far more than external events. In tennis, a bad call or a double fault is not what derails your match — it's your reaction that determines what happens next. By cultivating the habit of responding thoughtfully rather than impulsively, you maintain your poise and keep your mind clear for the next point. This discipline is what separates the mentally strong from the rest.

Actionable Insight: The next time something goes wrong in a match, pause, take a breath, and choose your response. Remind yourself: "My power lies in my reaction."

March 12
WELCOME THE UNEXPECTED

"To expect is to be disappointed. To accept is to be free."
— Seneca

Expectations can be a trap — when things don't go as you imagined, disappointment and frustration follow. The Stoics teach us to let go of rigid expectations and embrace whatever comes. In tennis, this means being ready for anything: a late opponent, a sudden rainstorm, or a surprising tactic. By welcoming the unexpected, you free yourself from disappointment and open yourself to creative solutions. This flexibility makes you a more resilient and dangerous competitor.

Actionable Insight: Before your next match, remind yourself: "I am ready for anything." When the unexpected happens, smile and adapt.

March 13
USE ADVERSITY TO BUILD CHARACTER

> "Difficulties are things that show a person what they are."
> — Epictetus

It's easy to be gracious and composed when everything is going well. True character is revealed in adversity. The Stoics believed that hardship is the ultimate test of who we are. In tennis, the way you handle a tough loss, a string of errors, or a hostile crowd says more about you than any victory. Use adversity as a mirror: let it show you where you are strong and where you need to grow.

 Actionable Insight: After your next difficult match, reflect on how you responded. Did you act with integrity and composure? Identify one area where you can strengthen your character.

March 14
FIND OPPORTUNITY IN EVERY LOSS

"Loss is nothing else but change, and change is Nature's delight."

— Marcus Aurelius

Every loss in tennis is a form of change — a shift in your record, your confidence, your perspective. The Stoics teach that change is not to be feared, but embraced as a source of growth and renewal. Each loss is an opportunity to analyze, adapt, and ultimately improve. By welcoming change, you turn setbacks into stepping stones and keep your progress moving forward.

Actionable Insight: After your next loss, write down three things you can change or improve in your game. Treat each loss as a catalyst for positive transformation.

March 15
PERSEVERANCE OVER PERFECTION

> "No one is ever unhappy because of someone else."
> — Seneca

It's tempting to blame others — opponents, coaches, referees — for our struggles. The Stoics remind us that our happiness and perseverance are our own responsibility. In tennis, the pursuit of perfection can lead to frustration and self-blame. Instead, focus on perseverance: showing up, working hard, and giving your best effort, regardless of setbacks or imperfections. This mindset leads to lasting fulfillment and steady improvement.

Actionable Insight: Set a goal for your next practice: focus on effort and perseverance, not perfection. If you catch yourself blaming others or circumstances, bring your attention back to what you can control.

March 16
ACCEPT THE ROLE YOU'RE GIVEN

> "Remember that you are an actor in a play, the playwright chooses the length of the play, and the role you will play."
> — Epictetus

You may not always get the role you want — a top seed, the home crowd, or the easier draw. The Stoics teach us to accept our place and play our part to the best of our ability. In tennis, this means embracing your current level, your unique strengths, and even your weaknesses. By accepting your role, you free yourself from envy and resentment, and you focus on making the most of every opportunity.

Actionable Insight: Before your next match, reflect on your unique journey and strengths. Embrace your current role and play it with pride and commitment.

March 17
THE GIFT OF ADVERSARIES

> "Difficulty shows what men are."
>
> — Epictetus

Facing tough opponents or challenging match situations is not a punishment, but a mirror. The Stoics believed that adversity reveals your true character and strengths. In tennis, the way you respond to a relentless rival or a string of lost points says more about you than any easy victory. Let each challenge show you where you are strong and where you need to grow. Instead of shrinking from adversity, meet it with curiosity and resolve — knowing that every test is a step toward mastery.

Actionable Insight: After your next match against a difficult opponent, reflect on your reactions and decisions. Write down one strength you discovered and one area for growth. Use this insight to guide your next week of practice.

March 18
DON'T ADD TO YOUR TROUBLES

> "He who fears death will never do anything worthy of a living man."
>
> — Seneca

Fear of failure, embarrassment, or loss can paralyze you on the court. The Stoics teach that fear — especially of things outside your control — only limits your potential. When you let go of imagined catastrophes and focus on playing boldly, you open yourself to growth and achievement. Courage is not the absence of fear, but the willingness to act in spite of it.

Actionable Insight: In your next match, identify one situation where fear usually holds you back (e.g., approaching the net, serving under pressure). Commit to facing it head-on, reminding yourself that playing boldly is more important than avoiding mistakes.

March 19
THE VIRTUE OF ENDURANCE

> "He is a wise man who does not grieve for the things which he has not, but rejoices for those which he has."
> — Epictetus

Endurance is not just about physical stamina, but about gratitude and perspective. The Stoics teach us to appreciate what we have — our health, our chance to play, our progress — rather than lamenting what's missing. In tennis, this means finding joy in the process, even when results aren't immediate. Endurance fueled by gratitude is sustainable and uplifting.

Actionable Insight: After your next practice, write down three things you're grateful for in your tennis journey. Let this gratitude fuel your endurance through tough times.

March 20
TURN CRITICISM INTO FUEL

> "If anyone tells you that a certain person speaks ill of you, do not make excuses about what is said of you but answer: 'He was ignorant of my other faults, else he would not have mentioned these alone.'"
>
> — Epictetus

Criticism — whether from coaches, opponents, or spectators — can sting. The Stoics teach us to accept criticism with humility and even humor. In tennis, use feedback (even harsh or unfair) as fuel for improvement. If it's true, let it guide your growth; if it's not, let it go. This approach keeps you focused on learning rather than defending your ego.

 Actionable Insight: The next time you receive criticism, thank the person (even silently), reflect on what you can learn, and move forward without resentment.

March 21
LET GO OF WHAT YOU CAN'T CONTROL

> "Make the best use of what is in your power, and take the rest as it happens."
>
> — Epictetus

There will always be things outside your control in tennis — weather, officiating, your opponent's behavior. The Stoics teach us to focus on what we can influence and accept the rest. This mindset frees you from frustration and allows you to channel your energy into productive action.

 Actionable Insight: Before your next match, list what is in your control and what is not. Commit to letting go of the latter and giving your best to the former.

March 22
KEEP MOVING FORWARD

"How long are you going to wait before you demand the best for yourself?"

— Epictetus

Improvement requires action, not just intention. The Stoics urge us to stop waiting for perfect conditions and start pursuing excellence now. In tennis, this means pushing yourself in every practice, seeking feedback, and setting higher standards. Don't wait for the "right time" — make today the day you demand more of yourself.

 Actionable Insight: Set one ambitious but achievable goal for your next week of tennis. Take the first step today, no matter how small.

March 23
FIND CALM IN THE STORM

> "If you are calm while those around you are losing their heads, you will win."
>
> — MARCUS AURELIUS
> (PARAPHRASED)

Pressure situations — tiebreaks, match points, hostile crowds — are where calmness is most valuable. The Stoics believed that tranquility is a sign of strength. In tennis, the player who can remain composed under stress gains a decisive advantage. Calmness allows you to think clearly, execute your shots, and seize opportunities while others falter.

Actionable Insight: Practice calming techniques — deep breathing, visualizing a peaceful place — before and during your next high-pressure match.

March 24
THE POWER OF ROUTINE

> "Excellence is not an act, but a habit."
>
> — ARISTOTLE
> (STOIC-ADJACENT)

Greatness in tennis isn't achieved through occasional brilliance, but through consistent routines and habits. The Stoics understood that daily practice, reflection, and preparation are what build resilience and skill. By establishing strong routines — whether it's your warm-up, your mental preparation, or your post-match review — you create a foundation that supports you in the toughest moments.

Actionable Insight: Review your tennis routines. Identify one habit you can improve or make more consistent this week, and notice how it impacts your performance.

March 25
USE SETBACKS AS STEPPING STONES

> "He is a wise man who does not grieve for the things which he has not, but rejoices for those which he has."
>
> — EPICTETUS

Setbacks in tennis — whether it's a tough loss, an injury, or a missed opportunity — can easily lead to frustration. The Stoics remind us that wisdom lies in appreciating what you do have: your health, your ability to compete, your progress so far. By focusing on gratitude rather than what's lacking, you transform obstacles into opportunities for growth and renewed motivation. Each challenge becomes a chance to build resilience and to celebrate the journey, not just the outcome.

Actionable Insight: After your next setback, write down three aspects of your tennis journey you're grateful for. Let this gratitude shift your mindset from disappointment to determination, and use it as fuel to move forward.

March 26
CELEBRATE SMALL WINS

> "If you want to improve, be content to be thought foolish and stupid."
>
> — Epictetus

Improvement in tennis often means starting from scratch, making mistakes, and risking embarrassment as you try new things. The Stoics teach that progress requires humility — the willingness to look awkward in pursuit of growth. When you focus on steady improvement rather than how you appear to others, you lay the groundwork for real change. Each small, imperfect step is a necessary part of the journey, and over time, these steps add up to significant transformation.

 Actionable Insight: This week, deliberately work on a weakness, even if it feels uncomfortable or exposes your inexperience. Embrace the discomfort as evidence that you're on the path to improvement.

March 27
PRACTICE DETACHMENT

"Receive without pride, let go without attachment."
— Marcus Aurelius

Wins and losses are fleeting. The Stoics teach us to enjoy success without arrogance and to accept defeat without despair. In tennis, this means playing with passion but not letting results define your identity. Detachment allows you to stay balanced, focused, and resilient, no matter the outcome.

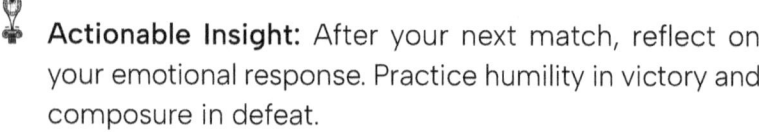 **Actionable Insight:** After your next match, reflect on your emotional response. Practice humility in victory and composure in defeat.

March 28
THE WISDOM OF REFLECTION

"Self-examination is the key to insight."

— SOCRATES

(STOIC-ADJACENT)

The Stoics practiced daily reflection to learn from every experience. In tennis, honest self-examination after each match or practice helps you spot patterns, correct mistakes, and reinforce what works. By making reflection a regular part of your routine, you turn every setback into a lesson and every success into a stepping stone for further growth.

Actionable Insight: After each session, spend five minutes reflecting on what you learned — about your game, your mindset, and your habits. Use these insights to set a goal for your next practice.

March 29
PROGRESS, NOT PERFECTION

> "Better to trip with the feet than with the tongue."
> — Zeno of Citium

In tennis, mistakes on the court — missed shots, double faults, tactical errors — are inevitable and part of the learning process. The Stoics remind us that it's far more productive to accept these physical missteps than to let negative self-talk or harsh criticism take over. What you say to yourself after an error matters more than the error itself. Instead of berating yourself, treat each mistake as a lesson and move forward with composure and focus. By managing your internal dialogue, you build resilience and keep your confidence intact, which is essential for long-term improvement and enjoyment of the game.

Actionable Insight: During your next practice or match, notice your self-talk after a mistake. Replace any negative comment with a constructive one (e.g., "I'll adjust my timing next time" instead of "That was terrible"). Make it your goal to respond to every error with encouragement and curiosity, not criticism.

March 30
THE JOURNEY IS THE REWARD

> "To live a good life: We have the potential for it. If we learn to be indifferent to what makes no difference."
> — Marcus Aurelius

The Stoics remind us that fulfillment comes from the journey, not the destination. In tennis, the daily practice, the friendships, the lessons learned — all are part of the reward. By focusing on what truly matters and letting go of trivial concerns, you find deeper satisfaction in your tennis life.

Actionable Insight: Reflect on what you love most about your tennis journey. Make time to appreciate the process, the people, and the growth, not just the results.

March 31
BEGIN AGAIN

> "Every day is a new beginning. Take a deep breath and start again."
>
> — UNKNOWN

The Stoics teach that each day, each match, and each point is a fresh start. No matter what happened yesterday, you have the opportunity to begin again with renewed focus and intention. In tennis, this means letting go of past mistakes and approaching every new challenge with curiosity and determination.

Actionable Insight: Before your next match or practice, take a moment to breathe deeply and set a clear intention for the session. Treat each point as a new beginning, regardless of past results.

March Wrap-Up

THIS MONTH, YOU learned to see every obstacle as a chance to grow stronger, wiser, and more resilient. By meeting adversity with acceptance and determination, you've begun to turn setbacks into stepping stones and challenges into opportunities. Carry this mindset forward — let each difficulty reveal your true character and fuel your progress, both on and off the court.

April Theme

Stoic Clarity — Mastering Perception and the Power of Thought

April's theme is the Stoic mastery of perception — the art of seeing clearly, thinking wisely, and directing your mind to what matters most. In tennis, as in life, your thoughts shape your reality. By learning to control your perceptions, you unlock resilience, focus, and joy on the court, no matter what circumstances arise.

April 1
THE HAPPINESS OF YOUR LIFE DEPENDS ON YOUR THOUGHTS

> "Your mind will take the shape of what you frequently hold in thought."
>
> – Marcus Aurelius

The thoughts you entertain most often will shape your experience on court. If you focus on doubts or frustrations, your game will reflect that negativity. If you cultivate thoughts of resilience, learning, and gratitude, your tennis will flourish. The Stoics remind us that clarity and happiness start with the quality of our thoughts.

Actionable Insight: Before your next match, write down three positive thoughts or intentions. Refer to them whenever you notice your mind drifting toward negativity.

April 2
CONTROL YOUR PERCEPTIONS

> "Control your perceptions. Direct your actions properly. Willingly accept what's outside your control."
> – THE DAILY STOIC

Perception is the lens through which you see every moment on the court. Two players can face the same situation — say, a rain delay or a tough opponent — and have completely different experiences based on their perceptions. The Stoic practice is to notice your first reaction, step back, and choose a more objective, helpful perspective. By controlling your perception, you gain the power to respond rather than react, to stay calm under pressure, and to see opportunity where others see only obstacles.

 Actionable Insight: In your next match, when something unexpected happens, pause and ask: "How else could I see this?" Practice reframing setbacks as chances to grow.

April 3
THE SOUL BECOMES DYED WITH THE COLOR OF ITS THOUGHTS

> "The soul becomes dyed with the color of its thoughts."
> — MARCUS AURELIUS

Your habitual thoughts shape your character and your game. If you constantly criticize yourself, you'll play tense and fearful. If you foster patience, courage, and positivity, those qualities will infuse your tennis. The Stoics remind us that every thought is a brushstroke on the canvas of your soul. On the court, this means choosing thoughts that build confidence, resilience, and enjoyment. Over time, these thoughts become your default setting, coloring every aspect of your performance.

Actionable Insight: After each practice, reflect on the dominant thoughts you carried. Are they the colors you want to wear? If not, consciously choose new ones for tomorrow.

April 4
EXTERNAL THINGS ARE NOT THE PROBLEM

"External things are not the problem. It's your assessment of them. Which you can erase right now."
— Marcus Aurelius

It's easy to blame losses on conditions, opponents, or luck. But the Stoics teach that suffering comes from our judgment, not the event itself. The wind is just wind; a tough opponent is just another player. What matters is how you interpret and respond to these challenges. By erasing negative judgments and approaching each situation with curiosity and openness, you free yourself from unnecessary frustration and unlock your best tennis.

 Actionable Insight: The next time you catch yourself blaming something external, pause and ask: "Is this truly a problem, or just my judgment?" Practice letting go of unhelpful assessments.

April 5
THE QUALITY OF YOUR THOUGHTS SHAPES YOUR GAME

> "The universe is change; our life is what our thoughts make it."
>
> — Marcus Aurelius

Change is constant in tennis — momentum swings, evolving conditions, shifting emotions. The only constant is your mind. The Stoics urge us to recognize that your experience is shaped not by what happens, but by how you think about it. If you see change as threatening, you'll play with anxiety. If you see it as opportunity, you'll play with freedom.

Actionable Insight: During your next match, notice your thoughts when things change. Practice choosing thoughts that help you adapt and thrive in the face of uncertainty.

April 6
THE POWER OF THE PRESENT

> "True happiness is to enjoy the present, without anxious dependence upon the future."
> — Seneca

It's tempting to worry about the outcome of a match or dwell on what's next. But the Stoics remind us that only the present is real, and happiness is found by fully inhabiting it. On the court, this means letting go of past errors and future fears, and focusing on the point at hand. When you are present, you play with clarity, creativity, and joy.

Actionable Insight: Use a ritual — like bouncing the ball before a serve — to anchor yourself in the present. Whenever your mind wanders, gently bring it back to the here and now.

April 7
THE MIND IS UNCONQUERABLE

> "It is the power of the mind to be unconquerable."
>
> — Seneca

No matter how tough the opponent or difficult the conditions, your mind remains your final stronghold. The Stoics believed that true strength comes from within — a mind trained to remain steady, focused, and undisturbed. In tennis, this means refusing to be defeated by frustration, fatigue, or pressure. Your body may tire, but your mind can always choose resolve.

Actionable Insight: In your next tough match, repeat to yourself: "My mind is unconquerable." Notice how this mantra helps you dig deeper and stay composed.

April 8
THE DANGER OF COMPARISON

> "It never ceases to amaze me: we all love ourselves more than other people, but care more about their opinion than our own."
>
> – Marcus Aurelius

Comparing yourself to others — worrying about rankings, reputations, or what others think — only distracts you from your own progress. The Stoics warn against letting outside opinions govern your self-worth. On the court, focus on your own journey, your own values, and your own improvement. When you play for your own growth, you play with authenticity and freedom.

 Actionable Insight: Before your next match, set an intention to measure yourself only against your own goals and standards, not anyone else's.

Stoic Tennis

April 9
THE POWER OF SELF-REVIEW

"An unexamined life is not worth living."

— SOCRATES

Growth in tennis comes from honest self-examination. The Stoics and Socrates both advocated for regular review of your actions and mindset. By reflecting on your matches and practices, you identify strengths to build on and weaknesses to address, accelerating your improvement and deepening your understanding of yourself.

Actionable Insight: After each match, spend five minutes journaling about your performance and mindset. Use these insights to set a specific goal for your next session.

April 10
EMBRACE CHANGE

"Everything is change. Embrace that. Flow with it."
— The Daily Stoic

Tennis is a game of constant motion — no two points, matches, or seasons are ever the same. The Stoics teach us to welcome change as a natural part of life. Instead of resisting or fearing it, adapt and use it to your advantage. Flexibility is a hallmark of both great players and wise people.

Actionable Insight: During your next match, when something unexpected happens, consciously tell yourself: "This is an opportunity to adapt and grow." Notice how this mindset shift impacts your play.

April 11
THE PRESENT MOMENT IS ALL YOU POSSESS

> "No one ever loses a life other than the one they are living... The present moment lasts the same for all and is all anyone possesses."
>
> — MARCUS AURELIUS

Dwelling on the past or worrying about the future robs you of the only time you truly have: now. The Stoics urge us to live fully in the present, making the most of each moment. In tennis, this means focusing on the current point, the current breath, the current opportunity.

 Actionable Insight: Use each changeover as a cue to reset and return to the present. Remind yourself: "This point is all that matters right now."

April 12
THE FREEDOM OF LETTING GO

> "No person has the power to have everything they want, but it is in their power not to want what they don't have, and to cheerfully put to good use what they do have."
>
> – SENECA

Wanting things to be different — better weather, easier opponents, more wins — creates frustration and distraction. The Stoics teach that contentment comes from letting go of unnecessary desires and making the most of what you have. On the court, this means accepting your current skills, conditions, and opportunities, and giving your best with what's available.

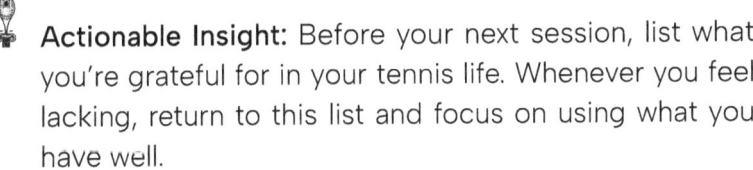 **Actionable Insight:** Before your next session, list what you're grateful for in your tennis life. Whenever you feel lacking, return to this list and focus on using what you have well.

April 13
THE MIND AS A GARDEN

> "Man is affected not by events, but by the view he takes of them."
>
> — Epictetus

Tennis is full of surprises — bad calls, net cords, unpredictable weather. The Stoics remind us that it's not the events themselves that determine your experience, but the perspective you bring. If you see every challenge as a personal affront, you'll play tense and frustrated. If you view them as opportunities to adapt and grow, you'll remain flexible and positive. Mastering your perspective is as important as mastering your strokes.

Actionable Insight: During your next match, when something unexpected happens, pause and ask: "How else can I see this?" Practice choosing a perspective that serves your growth and enjoyment.

April 14
SEE YOURSELF CLEARLY

"To know yourself is the beginning of wisdom."

— ARISTOTLE

(STOIC-ADJACENT)

True improvement in tennis starts with honest self-awareness. The Stoics and their contemporaries recognized that understanding your own strengths, weaknesses, and tendencies is essential for growth. On the court, this means noticing your habits under pressure, your emotional triggers, and the patterns in your play. By seeing yourself clearly — without harsh judgment or denial — you can make targeted changes that lead to real progress.

 Actionable Insight: After your next match or practice, jot down one strength and one weakness you noticed in your game. Choose one small adjustment to focus on in your next session. Over time, this habit of self-observation will sharpen your clarity and accelerate your improvement.

April 15
THE POWER OF SAYING NO

> "It may take some hard work. But the more you say no to the things that don't matter, the more you can say yes to the things that do."
>
> – THE DAILY STOIC

Distraction is the enemy of excellence. The Stoics teach the importance of discernment — choosing what to focus on and having the discipline to say no to what doesn't serve your purpose. In tennis, this means prioritizing your training, recovery, and mindset over distractions or temptations that pull you off course.

Actionable Insight: Identify one distraction you can eliminate this week. Use the time and energy you save to reinforce a habit that supports your tennis goals.

April 16
EMBRACE THE UNEXPECTED

> "Don't hope that events will turn out the way you want, welcome events in whichever way they happen: this is the path to peace."
>
> — Epictetus

In tennis, matches rarely unfold exactly as planned — your opponent might change tactics, the weather could shift, or you might not feel your best physically. The Stoic approach is not to cling to expectations, but to welcome whatever comes as an opportunity to adapt and grow. By embracing the unexpected, you free yourself from frustration and disappointment, and you become more resourceful on court. This attitude transforms every surprise — good or bad — into a chance to demonstrate resilience and creativity.

 Actionable Insight: Before your next match, remind yourself: "I am ready for anything." When something doesn't go as expected, pause, take a breath, and say, "I welcome this. I will adapt." Notice how this mindset shift helps you stay calm and focused, no matter what the game brings.

April 17
HUMILITY AS A FOUNDATION FOR GROWTH

> "If you wish to improve, be content to appear clueless or stupid in extraneous matters."
>
> — Epictetus

Improvement in tennis requires the humility to be a beginner, to make mistakes, and to ask questions. The Stoics teach that pride is an obstacle to learning; if you are too concerned with appearing skilled or knowledgeable, you'll shy away from situations that expose your weaknesses. On the court, this might mean working on a new grip that feels awkward, admitting you need help with your serve, or losing to a less experienced player because you're trying something new. Humility allows you to focus on the process of growth rather than the appearance of competence. This attitude not only accelerates your development but also makes you more receptive to coaching and feedback. Over time, those who are willing to look "clueless" in the short term become the most skilled in the long run.

 Actionable Insight: This week, deliberately put yourself in a learning situation that feels uncomfortable — take a lesson, try a new technique, or play with someone better than you. Embrace the awkwardness and focus on what you can learn, not how you appear.

April 18
THE POWER OF A STILL MIND

> "Nowhere can man find a quieter or more untroubled retreat than in his own soul."
>
> — Marcus Aurelius

Tennis matches can be chaotic — crowds, pressure, noise, and the relentless pace of play. Yet, the Stoics teach that you can always retreat to the quiet center of your own mind, no matter what is happening around you. This inner stillness is your refuge and your source of clarity. When you cultivate a calm mind, you are less likely to be rattled by an opponent's antics, a bad call, or a string of errors. Instead, you can pause, breathe, and return to your strategy with renewed focus. This ability to find stillness in the midst of chaos is what allows champions to play their best when it matters most. It's not about blocking out the world, but about creating a space within yourself where you can always find peace and perspective.

 Actionable Insight: Before and during your next match, practice a simple breathing exercise: inhale slowly for four counts, hold for four, exhale for four. Use this whenever you feel tension rising, and picture yourself retreating to a calm place within.

April 19
DON'T LET EMOTIONS CLOUD YOUR JUDGMENT

> "If you are pained by any external thing, it is not this thing that disturbs you, but your own judgment about it."
> — Marcus Aurelius

It's natural to feel a surge of emotion after a double fault, a missed opportunity, or a line call that goes against you. But the Stoics remind us that it's not the event itself that disturbs us, but our interpretation of it. If you let anger or disappointment take over, your judgment becomes clouded, leading to rash decisions and further mistakes. Clarity comes from recognizing your emotions without letting them dictate your actions. On court, this means pausing after a setback, acknowledging your feelings, and then choosing your next move with intention. By separating emotion from action, you maintain control over your game and prevent a single bad moment from becoming a downward spiral.

 Actionable Insight: In your next match, when you feel a strong emotion, pause for a brief moment before the next point. Name the feeling ("I'm frustrated" or "I'm anxious") and then ask, "What's the most constructive thing I can do right now?"

April 20
FOCUS ON THE FUNDAMENTALS

> "Do not be concerned with the things you cannot control; instead, devote yourself to what you can improve."
> — Epictetus

Tennis can become overwhelming when you try to manage every detail — your opponent's mood, the weather, the crowd, or even the outcome of each point. The Stoics remind us that peace and progress come from focusing on the basics: your footwork, your preparation, your attitude. When you direct your energy toward the fundamentals, you reduce anxiety and increase your consistency. Simplicity in your approach — trusting your training, repeating your routines, and playing your game — leads to clarity and better results, especially under pressure.

 Actionable Insight: Before your next match, write down the two or three most important fundamentals for your game (e.g., "Watch the ball," "Move my feet," "Stay positive"). Whenever you feel distracted or overwhelmed, return your attention to these basics and let everything else fade into the background.

April 21
THE FREEDOM OF DETACHMENT

> "Detachment is not that you should own nothing, but that nothing should own you."
>
> — ANONYMOUS

On the court, detachment means focusing on your process and effort, not obsessing over the scoreboard or your opponent's approval. It's about letting go of the need to prove yourself with every shot, and instead, embracing each point as an opportunity to learn and express your game. This mindset helps you recover from mistakes quickly, avoid emotional swings, and play with greater joy and creativity. You become more adaptable, less anxious, and better able to access your best tennis under pressure. Detachment allows you to honor the game, your opponent, and yourself, regardless of the result.

 Actionable Insight: This week, practice detachment by setting an intention before your matches or training:

- Remind yourself, "My value is not defined by the outcome of this match."
- Focus on your effort, attitude, and learning, rather than just the score.

April 22
THE IMPORTANCE OF SELF-HONESTY

> "Be not angry that you cannot make others as you wish them to be, since you cannot make yourself as you wish to be."
>
> – Thomas à Kempis
> (Stoic-adjacent)

It's easy to become frustrated with your opponent's behavior, the umpire's calls, or your coach's advice. But the Stoics remind us that we often struggle to shape even our own habits and attitudes, let alone control others. Self-honesty is the foundation of clarity: recognizing your own limitations, blind spots, and areas for growth. In tennis, this means being brutally honest about your weaknesses, your mindset, and your commitment. Only by seeing yourself clearly can you chart a course for real improvement.

Actionable Insight: After your next practice, ask yourself: "What did I avoid today? Where did I make excuses?" Write down one area where you can be more honest with yourself and set a plan to address it.

April 23
LEARN TO SEE CLEARLY THROUGH ERROR

> "To make no mistakes is not in the power of man; but from their errors and mistakes the wise and good learn wisdom for the future."
>
> — PLUTARCH

Mistakes on the court are inevitable. Whether it's a double fault at a key moment or a missed opportunity to close out a set, errors are part of every tennis journey. What separates great players is not perfection, but the ability to extract insight from imperfection. In Stoic philosophy, mistakes are raw material for reflection, not sources of shame. When you respond to errors with curiosity rather than judgment, you unlock clarity, resilience, and long-term growth.

 Actionable Insight: After your next match or practice, pick one mistake that frustrated you. Instead of brushing it off or berating yourself, ask: *"What did this reveal about my mindset, technique, or focus?"* Write down what you learned and how you'll approach it differently next time. Use mistakes as mirrors — not walls.

April 24
THE STRENGTH IN FLEXIBILITY

> "The wise adapt themselves to circumstances, as water molds itself to the pitcher."
>
> – Diogenes Laërtius
> (on Stoic adaptability)

Rigidity is the enemy of clarity. In tennis, conditions change constantly — weather, surfaces, opponents, even your own energy levels. The Stoics teach that wisdom lies in adaptability: the ability to adjust your mindset, tactics, or expectations in response to changing circumstances. Like water, you can flow around obstacles rather than being broken by them. This flexibility allows you to stay clear-headed and resourceful, turning unexpected challenges into opportunities for creativity and growth.

 Actionable Insight: In your next match, if something isn't working, pause and ask: "How can I adapt?" Experiment with a new tactic or mindset, and reflect afterward on what you learned from being flexible.

Stoic Tennis

April 25
THE DISCIPLINE OF ATTENTION

> "Pay attention to what's in front of you — the principle, the task, or what's being portrayed."
>
> — Marcus Aurelius

Distraction is everywhere — on the court and in life. The Stoics emphasize the discipline of attention: focusing fully on the task at hand, whether it's a practice drill, a crucial point, or a conversation with your coach. When your attention is scattered, your performance suffers and your experience is diminished. But when you bring your full awareness to the present, you unlock deeper learning, sharper execution, and greater satisfaction. Attention is a skill that must be trained, just like your serve or your footwork.

Actionable Insight: During your next practice, set a timer for ten minutes and commit to being fully present for that entire period — no checking your phone, no thinking about the score, just pure focus on the task. Gradually increase this time as your attention muscle grows.

April 26
THE WISDOM OF LETTING GO OF THE PAST

> "Don't let your reflection on the whole sweep of life crush you. Don't fill your mind with all the bad things that might still happen. Stay focused on the present situation and ask yourself why it's so unbearable and can't be survived."
> — Marcus Aurelius

It's easy to be haunted by past losses, embarrassing mistakes, or missed opportunities. The Stoics warn that dwelling on the past or fearing the future only clouds your mind and saps your energy. In tennis, clarity comes from letting go of what's behind you and focusing on the point at hand. Every new rally is a fresh start, every day a new chance to improve. By releasing the weight of the past, you free yourself to play with lightness, creativity, and courage.

Actionable Insight: After a tough match or practice, take a moment to acknowledge any lingering regrets. Then, visualize yourself setting them down, like a heavy bag, and walking forward unburdened. Practice this ritual whenever you feel stuck in the past.

April 27
THE COURAGE TO SEE THINGS AS THEY ARE

> "If someone is able to show me that what I think or do is not right, I will happily change, for I seek the truth by which no one was ever truly harmed."
>
> — Marcus Aurelius

Clarity requires the courage to face reality — even when it's uncomfortable. The Stoics valued truth over ego, always willing to change their minds or admit mistakes. In tennis, this means being open to feedback, willing to adjust your technique, and honest about your results. The more accurately you see your game, the faster you can improve. It takes courage to admit you need to change, but this is the path to mastery.

 Actionable Insight: Ask your coach or a trusted partner for honest feedback on your game. Listen without defensiveness, thank them, and choose one piece of advice to act on immediately.

April 28
THE LIBERATION OF ACCEPTANCE

> "Don't demand that things happen as you wish, but wish that they happen as they do, and your life will go smoothly."
> — Epictetus

Frustration often arises from the gap between expectation and reality. The Stoics teach that peace comes from accepting things as they are, not as you wish them to be. In tennis, this means embracing the match you have, not the one you imagined; the opponent you face, not the one you wanted. Acceptance is not resignation — it's the starting point for effective action. When you stop fighting reality, you can see clearly and respond wisely.

 Actionable Insight: The next time you catch yourself wishing something were different on court, pause and say: "Let me meet this moment as it is." Notice how acceptance opens the door to clarity and effective action.

April 29
THE STRENGTH OF CONSISTENCY

> "It is a rough road that leads to the heights of greatness."
> — SENECA

Consistency in tennis is not about perfection, but about showing up and putting in the work, day after day — even when progress feels slow or the path is challenging. Seneca reminds us that the journey to excellence is often difficult, and that's exactly what makes it meaningful. Every practice, every drill, and every match, no matter how tough, builds your foundation as a player. When you embrace the rough patches and keep moving forward, you develop the habits and resilience needed to reach your highest potential.

 Actionable Insight: During your next week of training, keep a simple log of your daily effort, no matter how small the improvement. At the end of the week, reflect on how your commitment through the "rough road" is already moving you closer to your tennis goals.

April 30
THE GIFT OF CLEAR VISION

"To see things as they are, not as you wish them to be, is the beginning of wisdom."

— Epictetus

The ultimate clarity is the ability to see reality — yourself, your game, your circumstances — without distortion or denial. The Stoics teach that wisdom begins with clear vision. In tennis, this means honestly assessing your strengths and weaknesses, recognizing what's working and what isn't, and making decisions based on facts, not fantasies. Clear vision allows you to set realistic goals, craft effective strategies, and respond to challenges with intelligence and grace.

 Actionable Insight: At the end of this month, review your tennis journey with honesty. What have you learned about yourself? What is the next step for your growth? Celebrate your clarity and set a new intention for May.

April Wrap-Up

APRIL HAS BEEN a month of sharpening your perception and mastering the power of thought. By learning to control your perspective, focus on the present, and let go of what you cannot control, you've built greater clarity and resilience on and off the court. Carry this mental clarity forward, using it as a foundation for wise decisions, steady emotions, and consistent growth in your tennis journey.

May Theme

Virtue in Action — Building Character On and Off the Court

THE STOICS BELIEVED that virtue — qualities like courage, justice, temperance, and wisdom — was the highest good and the key to a meaningful life. In tennis, as in life, your character is revealed not just by how you play, but by how you conduct yourself: how you handle adversity, treat opponents, and pursue excellence. This month, we'll explore how Stoic virtue can elevate your tennis and your life.

May 1
THE FOUNDATION OF VIRTUE

"If it is not right, do not do it; if it is not true, do not say it."
— MARCUS AURELIUS

Integrity is the bedrock of both Stoicism and sportsmanship. On the court, you are constantly faced with choices: whether to make an honest line call, whether to respect your opponent, whether to own up to your mistakes. The Stoics teach that right action is not determined by convenience or what others do, but by your own unwavering commitment to what is just and true. When you choose integrity, you build trust with others and, more importantly, with yourself. This self-trust translates into greater confidence under pressure, because you know you stand on solid ground. Virtue is not just about grand gestures, but about the small, everyday choices that define your character.

Actionable Insight: In your next match, make it your highest priority to act with complete honesty and fairness, especially when no one else is watching. Notice how this commitment affects your mindset and your respect for yourself.

May 2
COURAGE IN THE FACE OF FEAR

> "You will encounter many defeats, but you must not be defeated."
>
> — Maya Angelou
> (Stoic-adjacent)

Fear is a constant companion in tennis — fear of losing, of making mistakes, of not living up to expectations. The Stoics saw courage not as the absence of fear, but as the willingness to act in spite of it. Every time you step onto the court, you have the chance to practice courage: to go for your shots under pressure, to face a stronger opponent, to bounce back after a tough loss. Courage is a muscle that grows with use. By embracing challenges and refusing to shrink from discomfort, you become not just a better player, but a braver person.

 Actionable Insight: Identify one situation in tennis that scares you — perhaps playing a higher-ranked opponent or serving at match point. This week, seek out that challenge and approach it with the mindset: "I choose courage over comfort."

May 3
THE POWER OF TEMPERANCE

> "Self-control is strength. Right thought is mastery. Calmness is power."
>
> — JAMES ALLEN
> (STOIC-ADJACENT)

Tennis rewards not just physical strength, but emotional mastery. When you can stay composed in chaos, resist frustration after an error, or dial down adrenaline to execute your strategy, you're practicing temperance — the Stoic virtue of self-control. This quote from James Allen distills the path to mastery: first manage your thoughts, then your emotions, and the body will follow. Temperance helps you stay sharp in a tiebreaker, patient in long rallies, and humble after both victory and defeat. It creates the space where power meets purpose.

Actionable Insight: Choose one on-court impulse you often battle — rushing, complaining, over-hitting. During your next match, practice pausing and taking a deep breath when that impulse arises. Use the mantra: *"Calm is power."* Track how often you successfully respond with control rather than reaction.

May 4
JUSTICE — TREATING OTHERS FAIRLY

> "Wherever there is a human being, there is an opportunity for kindness."
>
> — Seneca

Justice, for the Stoics, means treating others with fairness, respect, and compassion. Tennis is a competitive sport, but it is also a community. How you treat your opponent, your doubles partner, the officials, and even the ball kids reflects your character. Acts of kindness — congratulating an opponent on a good shot, helping a new player, or accepting a close call with grace — build a culture of respect and elevate the game for everyone. Justice is not just about following the rules, but about honoring the spirit of the game and the dignity of every person you encounter.

Actionable Insight: In your next match or practice, look for opportunities to show kindness and fairness, especially in small moments. Notice how this affects your mood and the atmosphere around you.

May 5
WISDOM — LEARNING FROM EVERY EXPERIENCE

> "It is impossible for a man to learn what he thinks he already knows."
>
> — Epictetus

Wisdom is the ability to learn from every situation, to remain open and curious, and to seek truth over ego. In tennis, this means approaching every match, win or lose, as a lesson. The Stoics remind us that arrogance is the enemy of growth; the moment you think you know it all, you stop improving. True wisdom is humble and hungry: it asks, "What can I learn from this opponent, this mistake, this victory?" By adopting the mindset of a lifelong learner, you transform every experience into fuel for your development.

Actionable Insight: After each session this week, write down one thing you learned — about your game, your mindset, or yourself. Share your insight with a coach or teammate to reinforce your learning.

May 6
THE VIRTUE OF GRATITUDE

> "Contentment comes not so much from great wealth as from few wants."
>
> – Epictetus

Gratitude and contentment are powerful antidotes to frustration and envy. The Stoics remind us that happiness is found in appreciating what you have, rather than longing for what you lack. In tennis, this means valuing your progress, your health, and the opportunity to play, instead of fixating on rankings or results. Contentment fuels motivation and resilience.

 Actionable Insight: Before each practice, list three things you're grateful for in your tennis journey. Let this sense of abundance inspire your effort and enjoyment.

May 7
HUMILITY — THE PATH TO MASTERY

> "If anyone tells you that a certain person speaks ill of you, do not make excuses about what is said of you but answer: 'He was ignorant of my other faults, else he would not have mentioned these alone.'"
>
> — EPICTETUS

Humility is the recognition that you are always a work in progress. The Stoics teach that criticism is inevitable, but it is also an opportunity for self-examination and growth. In tennis, humility means being open to feedback, admitting your mistakes, and recognizing that you always have more to learn. It's about putting the pursuit of excellence above the need for praise or the fear of judgment. Humility keeps your ego in check and your mind open, allowing you to grow faster and connect more deeply with others.

Actionable Insight: When you receive criticism or feedback this week, thank the person sincerely and reflect on what you can learn from it. Practice humility by seeking out advice from those who know more than you.

May 8
PERSEVERANCE — ENDURING WITH PURPOSE

> "Endure and persist; this pain will turn to good by and by."
> – Ovid
> (Stoic-adjacent)

Perseverance is the virtue of continuing in the face of obstacles, setbacks, and pain. The Stoics saw endurance not as mere suffering, but as purposeful action — persisting because you believe in your goal and your values. In tennis, perseverance is what gets you through tough training blocks, long matches, and periods of self-doubt. It's the quiet strength that keeps you moving forward, trusting that every struggle is shaping you into a stronger, wiser competitor.

 **Actionable Insight:** The next time you feel like quitting — whether in a drill, a match, or your training — remind yourself of your purpose. Take one more step, play one more point, and celebrate your perseverance.

May 9
THE JOY OF EXCELLENCE

"Pleasure in the job puts perfection in the work."

— Aristotle
(Stoic-adjacent)

Virtue is not just about duty; it's about finding joy in the pursuit of excellence. The Stoics believed that living in accordance with virtue brings a deep, lasting happiness. In tennis, this means taking pride in your effort, your preparation, and your sportsmanship, regardless of the outcome. When you focus on the process and the values you bring to the court, you experience a sense of fulfillment that goes beyond wins and losses. Excellence becomes its own reward.

Actionable Insight: This week, choose one aspect of your tennis — footwork, serve, attitude — and commit to doing it with excellence and enjoyment. Notice how this focus elevates your entire game.

May 10
LIVING YOUR VALUES

"Waste no more time arguing what a good man should be. Be one."

— Marcus Aurelius

It's easy to talk about values — honesty, respect, courage — but the Stoics challenge us to embody them in every action. On the tennis court, this means letting your behavior reflect your ideals, especially when it's difficult. Whether it's calling your own lines, shaking hands after a heated match, or supporting a struggling teammate, your actions reveal your true character. Living your values is not always easy, but it is always within your control. When you do, you inspire others and build a legacy that lasts far beyond any trophy.

Actionable Insight: Choose one core value you want to embody on court this week. Write it on your wristband, your racquet, or in your journal. At the end of each day, reflect on how well you lived up to it and where you can improve.

May 11
THE VIRTUE OF PATIENCE

> "No great thing is created suddenly."
>
> — EPICTETUS

Patience is the quiet force behind every achievement in tennis. Improvement is rarely linear; there are plateaus, setbacks, and moments when progress seems invisible. The Stoics remind us that anything of value — whether it's a strong serve, a resilient mindset, or a reputation for fairness — takes time and steady effort. On the court, impatience leads to frustration, rushed decisions, and giving up too soon. Patience, on the other hand, allows you to trust the process, to keep showing up, and to celebrate small gains. Over months and years, patience transforms effort into excellence.

 Actionable Insight: Pick one area of your game that's slow to improve. Commit to a daily or weekly practice, and measure progress in small increments. When impatience arises, remind yourself: "No great thing is created suddenly."

May 12
GENEROSITY — GIVING WITHOUT EXPECTATION

> "Remember that you are here not to be served, but to serve."
>
> — Marcus Aurelius

Tennis can be an individual pursuit, but the Stoics teach the virtue of generosity — giving your time, energy, and encouragement to others without expecting anything in return. This could mean mentoring a younger player, volunteering at a tournament, or simply offering a kind word to a struggling teammate. Generosity builds community, strengthens character, and reminds you that the value of tennis goes far beyond personal achievement.

 Actionable Insight: This week, look for an opportunity to give something to your tennis community — your time, knowledge, or support. Reflect on how this act of service enriches your own experience.

May 13
THE STRENGTH TO FORGIVE

> "The best revenge is to be unlike him who performed the injury."
>
> — MARCUS AURELIUS

Conflict is inevitable in competitive sports. You may encounter opponents who cheat, coaches who criticize unfairly, or teammates who let you down. The Stoic response is not to seek revenge or harbor resentment, but to rise above and act with integrity. Forgiveness is not weakness; it is the strength to let go of anger and reclaim your peace. On the court, this means moving on quickly from slights, treating others with respect regardless of their actions, and focusing on your own conduct.

Actionable Insight: If you're holding onto resentment — over a bad call, a harsh word, or a betrayal — take a moment to acknowledge it. Then, consciously choose to let it go and focus on your own values.

May 14
DISCIPLINE BUILDS INTEGRITY

> "Do not explain your philosophy. Embody it."
>
> – Epictetus

Marcus Aurelius' advice is a blueprint for virtuous competition. It's easy to expect perfection from others — teammates, opponents, or officials — but Stoic excellence comes from focusing inward. Hold yourself to a high standard: in how you train, how you behave under pressure, and how you speak to yourself. At the same time, extend patience and empathy toward others. That balance creates a competitive mindset grounded in accountability and respect.

Actionable Insight: For your next match or training session, set a personal code of conduct (e.g., no negative self-talk, hustle for every ball, accept calls with grace). Then, when others falter or frustrate you, respond with composure — not criticism. Character shows in contrast.

May 15
THE VIRTUE OF MODESTY

> "Let another praise you, and not your own mouth."
>
> — Proverbs
> (Stoic-adjacent)

Success can tempt you to boast or seek validation, but the Stoics valued modesty — a quiet confidence that needs no external applause. In tennis, let your actions and attitude speak for themselves. Celebrate your victories with humility and gratitude, and remember that every achievement rests on the support of coaches, teammates, and even worthy opponents. Modesty keeps your ego in check and your focus on continual improvement.

 Actionable Insight: After your next win or compliment, simply say "thank you" and shift your attention to your next goal. Notice how this modesty deepens your satisfaction and relationships.

May 16
THE WISDOM OF LISTENING

> "We have two ears and one mouth, so that we can listen twice as much as we speak."
> — Epictetus

Listening is an underrated virtue in both tennis and life. Whether it's absorbing a coach's advice, understanding a partner's perspective, or tuning in to your own body's signals, listening opens the door to wisdom. The Stoics believed that true knowledge begins with humility and the willingness to learn from everyone. On the court, the best players are those who are always learning — by watching, by asking, and by truly listening.

 Actionable Insight: In your next lesson or practice, focus on listening more than speaking. Afterward, jot down one new thing you learned simply by paying closer attention.

May 17
COMPASSION — SEEING YOURSELF AND OTHERS CLEARLY

> "Whenever you are about to find fault with someone, ask yourself the following question: What fault of mine most nearly resembles the one I am about to criticize?"
> — MARCUS AURELIUS

It's easy to criticize others — an opponent's gamesmanship, a partner's missed shot, a coach's tough feedback. But the Stoics urge us to look inward first, recognizing our own imperfections. Compassion is not just kindness, but the wisdom to see yourself and others as fellow travelers on the same journey of growth. In tennis, this means forgiving mistakes, offering encouragement, and treating everyone with empathy. This approach not only makes you a better teammate but also helps you handle your own setbacks with greater grace.

Actionable Insight: The next time you feel critical of someone on court, pause and ask: "Have I ever done the same?" Use this moment to practice compassion and understanding.

May 18
THE VALUE OF FRIENDSHIP

"One loyal friend is worth ten thousand relatives."
— Euripides
(Stoic-adjacent)

Tennis can be a solitary sport, but the relationships you build — coaches, hitting partners, rivals who become friends — are one of its greatest rewards. The Stoics valued friendship as a source of support, challenge, and joy. A true friend on the court will push you to improve, celebrate your victories, and help you through defeats. Nurture these relationships with honesty, generosity, and loyalty, and your tennis journey will be richer for it.

 Actionable Insight: Reach out to a tennis friend or mentor this week. Thank them for their support, and look for a way to strengthen your bond — whether it's a practice session, a note of encouragement, or simply sharing your gratitude.

May 19
THE STRENGTH OF ADAPTABILITY

> "The wise man adapts himself to circumstances as water shapes itself to the vessel that contains it."
>
> — SENECA

Adaptability is a hallmark of both great players and wise people. Conditions change — wind, surfaces, opponents' tactics, even your own energy levels. The Stoics teach that wisdom lies in flexibility: the ability to adjust your approach without losing sight of your purpose. On court, this means being willing to change your strategy, to try new things, and to stay open to learning. The more adaptable you are, the more resilient and resourceful you become, able to turn any circumstance to your advantage.

 Actionable Insight: In your next match, deliberately try a new tactic or adjust your game plan if things aren't working. Reflect afterward on what you learned from being flexible.

May 20
THE VIRTUE OF DILIGENCE

> "Freedom is the only worthy goal in life. It is won by disregarding things that lie beyond our control."
> — EPICTETUS

Diligence in tennis means focusing your energy on what you can control — your effort, attitude, and preparation. The Stoics teach that wisdom lies in distinguishing between what is up to us and what is not. When you stop worrying about your opponent's skill or the weather and instead channel your diligence into your own training and mindset, you give yourself the best chance to succeed.

 Actionable Insight: Before your next match, list three things you can control and three you cannot. During play, use this list to refocus your attention on your preparation and effort whenever you feel distracted by externals.

May 21
THE PEACE OF ACCEPTANCE

> "He is a wise man who yields to the inevitable."
>
> — EURIPIDES
> (STOIC-ADJACENT)

There are times in tennis when, despite your best efforts, things don't go your way — an injury, a rainout, a tough loss. The Stoics teach that peace comes from accepting what you cannot change and focusing on what you can. Acceptance is not giving up; it's the wisdom to let go of resistance and channel your energy into constructive action. This mindset frees you from bitterness and helps you bounce back stronger.

Actionable Insight: After your next disappointment, take a moment to acknowledge your feelings. Then, ask: "What can I do now?" Shift your focus from what's lost to what's possible.

May 22
THE POWER OF REFLECTION

"Let us examine our thoughts; let us examine our actions; let us examine our desires."

— Seneca

Self-reflection is the engine of growth. The Stoics practiced daily examination of their thoughts, actions, and motivations. In tennis, regular reflection helps you identify patterns, correct mistakes, and reinforce positive habits. It's not about self-criticism, but about honest assessment and intentional improvement. The more you reflect, the more you learn — and the faster you grow.

Actionable Insight: Set aside ten minutes at the end of each week to review your tennis: What went well? What needs work? What did you learn about yourself? Use these insights to set goals for the week ahead.

May 23
THE JOY OF SERVICE

"The fruit of service is peace."

— MARCUS AURELIUS

Serving others — whether it's helping a teammate, volunteering at an event, or coaching a beginner — brings a sense of fulfillment that personal achievement alone cannot match. The Stoics believed that contributing to the greater good is a key part of a virtuous life. In tennis, service connects you to your community, gives purpose to your efforts, and reminds you that the game is bigger than any one player.

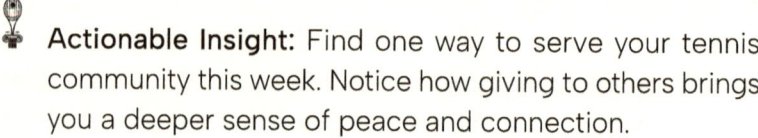

Actionable Insight: Find one way to serve your tennis community this week. Notice how giving to others brings you a deeper sense of peace and connection.

May 24
THE VALUE OF CONSISTENCY

> "Practice yourself, for heaven's sake, in little things; and thence proceed to greater."
>
> — Epictetus

Mastery is built on the foundation of daily practice and attention to detail. The Stoics remind us that greatness is the result of consistent effort in small things. In tennis, this means focusing on your routines, refining your technique, and building habits that support your goals. Over time, these small acts of discipline add up to significant transformation.

 Actionable Insight: Choose one small habit to reinforce this month — such as a daily warm-up routine or post-match reflection. Track your consistency and celebrate your commitment to growth.

May 25
THE WISDOM OF DETACHMENT

> "To live a good life: We have the potential for it. If we learn to be indifferent to what makes no difference."
> – Marcus Aurelius

Not everything in tennis — or life — deserves your emotional investment. The Stoics teach the wisdom of detachment: caring deeply about what matters (your effort, your values, your growth), and letting go of what doesn't (gossip, criticism, things outside your control). Detachment allows you to stay focused, calm, and resilient, no matter what swirls around you.

Actionable Insight: This week, notice when you get caught up in things that don't truly matter. Practice letting them go and redirect your attention to what's truly important.

May 26
THE VIRTUE OF HOPE

> "Dwell on the beauty of life. Watch the stars, and see yourself running with them."
>
> — Marcus Aurelius

Hope is not wishful thinking, but the virtue of seeing possibility even in difficulty. The Stoics remind us to appreciate the beauty and wonder of life, even as we strive for improvement. In tennis, hope keeps you motivated through tough times, fuels your dreams, and helps you see every challenge as a new opportunity. Hope is the light that guides you forward, no matter how dark the path may seem.

Actionable Insight: After a tough session, take a moment to reflect on what you love about tennis and what you hope to achieve. Let this hope inspire your next step.

May 27
THE POWER OF EXAMPLE

> "Don't explain your philosophy. Embody it."
>
> — Epictetus

Words are powerful, but actions are even more so. The Stoics believed that the best way to teach virtue is to live it. On the court, your behavior — how you handle pressure, how you treat others, how you respond to setbacks — sets an example for everyone around you. When you embody your values, you inspire others to do the same, creating a ripple effect of excellence and integrity.

 Actionable Insight: This week, choose one value you want to model — such as respect, perseverance, or humility. Focus on living it fully, and notice how others respond to your example.

May 28
THE STRENGTH OF COMMUNITY

> "We are made for cooperation, like feet, like hands, like eyelids, like the rows of the upper and lower teeth."
> — Marcus Aurelius

Even in an individual sport, your success is built on the support of others — coaches, partners, family, and friends. The Stoics saw humans as social beings, meant to work together for the common good. In tennis, fostering a spirit of cooperation — sharing knowledge, supporting teammates, and celebrating others' successes — makes everyone stronger. Community is a source of resilience, motivation, and joy.

Actionable Insight: Reach out to someone in your tennis community and offer support or encouragement. Reflect on how your connections enrich your tennis journey.

May 29
THE VIRTUE OF CHEERFULNESS

> "A cheerful heart is a good medicine."
> — PROVERBS (STOIC-ADJACENT)

Cheerfulness is the ability to maintain a positive, light-hearted spirit, even in adversity. The Stoics valued joy as a sign of wisdom — a recognition that life, and tennis, are gifts to be enjoyed. A cheerful player lifts the spirits of those around them, bounces back from setbacks more quickly, and finds fulfillment in the journey.

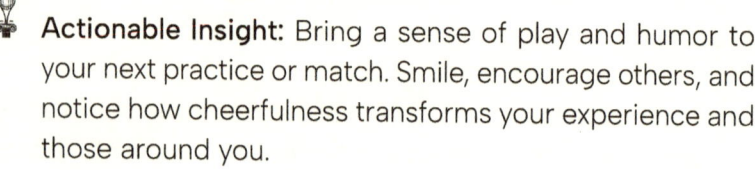

Actionable Insight: Bring a sense of play and humor to your next practice or match. Smile, encourage others, and notice how cheerfulness transforms your experience and those around you.

May 30
THE LEGACY OF CHARACTER

"Character is fate."

— Heraclitus (Stoic-adjacent)

Your skills and achievements may fade, but your character endures. The Stoics believed that who you become is ultimately your destiny. In tennis, your legacy is not just your record, but the way you played the game — the respect you showed, the effort you gave, the example you set. Every day on court is a chance to build a legacy of integrity, courage, and kindness.

 Actionable Insight: Reflect on the legacy you want to leave in your tennis community. What do you want others to remember about you? Let this vision guide your actions today.

May 31
ACCEPT YOUR FATE AND PLAY ON

> "Lead me, Zeus, and you, Fate, wherever you have assigned me. I shall follow without hesitation; but even if I am unwilling, because I am wretched, I shall follow nonetheless."
>
> — Cleanthes

Every tennis match brings surprises — bad bounces, tough draws, unexpected weather, or an opponent playing the match of their life. Cleanthes, the second head of the Stoic school, reminds us that true wisdom lies in accepting whatever fate brings, willingly or not. On the court, this means embracing the conditions, the opponent, and the outcome, whether or not they match your hopes. By following the path laid out for you with resolve and openness, you free yourself from frustration and play your best tennis, no matter what arises.

 Actionable Insight: Before your next match, take a moment to acknowledge anything out of your control — be it the weather, the draw, or your opponent's style. Say to yourself, "I accept what comes, and I will give my best regardless." Notice how this acceptance brings you calm and helps you focus on your effort and attitude, not just the result.

May Wrap-Up

In May, you explored how virtue shapes your tennis and your character — on and off the court. By practicing courage, integrity, patience, humility, and self-discipline, you've strengthened not just your game, but your sense of purpose and resilience. Carry these virtues forward, letting them guide your actions and decisions as you continue to grow as both a competitor and a person.

June Theme

Resilience and Endurance — Weathering the Storms

T̲ʜᴇ Sᴛᴏɪᴄs ʙᴇʟɪᴇᴠᴇᴅ that true greatness is revealed not in comfort, but in adversity. Resilience — the ability to endure hardship, rebound from setbacks, and keep moving forward no matter what — is a defining trait of both the Stoic sage and the champion athlete. This month, we'll explore how to cultivate unshakable endurance and resilience on and off the court.

June 1
THE ART OF ENDURANCE

> "Endurance is one of the most difficult disciplines, but it is to the one who endures that the final victory comes."
> — BUDDHA
> (STOIC-ADJACENT)

Endurance is more than physical stamina; it's the mental and emotional strength to keep going when the match gets tough, when fatigue sets in, or when you're down in the score. The Stoics saw endurance as a noble discipline — a willingness to bear discomfort, to persist through pain, and to remain steadfast in the face of obstacles. In tennis, endurance is what carries you through long rallies, grueling tournaments, and the inevitable ups and downs of improvement. By embracing endurance as a virtue, you learn to welcome challenges as opportunities to build your strength, knowing that each trial brings you closer to your goals.

 Actionable Insight: During your next tough session or match, when you feel the urge to quit, repeat to yourself: "Endure, and the victory will be mine." Notice how this mindset shift helps you push through barriers.

June 2
THE POWER OF PERSEVERANCE

> "How long are you going to wait before you demand the best for yourself?"
>
> — EPICTETUS

Resilience is not just about surviving adversity, but about persisting in the pursuit of excellence, day after day. The Stoics challenge us to stop waiting for perfect conditions and to start striving for our best right now. In tennis, perseverance means showing up for every practice, giving your all in every drill, and refusing to be discouraged by setbacks. The journey to mastery is long and filled with obstacles, but each step forward, no matter how small, builds your capacity for greatness.

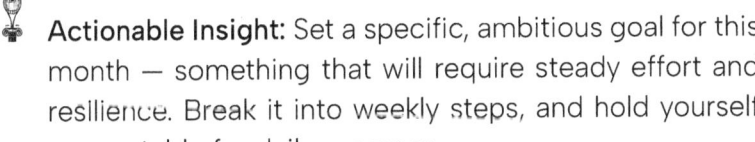 **Actionable Insight:** Set a specific, ambitious goal for this month — something that will require steady effort and resilience. Break it into weekly steps, and hold yourself accountable for daily progress.

June 3
STRENGTH LIES IN HOW YOU RESPOND

> "It's not things themselves that disturb us, but our opinions about them."
>
> — Epictetus

On the court, setbacks are inevitable: a bad call, a missed shot, or an unexpected error. The Stoics remind us that it's not the event itself that determines your experience, but how you interpret it. If you view a mistake as a catastrophe, frustration and self-doubt will follow. If you see it as a chance to learn and refocus, you maintain your composure and give yourself the best chance to recover. Your response — not the setback — shapes your match and your growth as a player.

 Actionable Insight: In your next practice or match, when something goes wrong, pause and ask yourself: "What story am I telling myself about this?" Reframe the moment as an opportunity to reset and improve, and notice how this shift affects your performance.

June 4
THE STRENGTH OF ADAPTABILITY

> "The wise adapt themselves to circumstances as water molds itself to the pitcher."
>
> — DIOGENES LAËRTIUS
> (ON STOIC ADAPTABILITY)

Resilience is not just about standing firm; it's also about bending without breaking. Conditions change — weather, opponents, even your own body. The Stoics valued adaptability: the ability to adjust your tactics, mindset, or expectations in response to new challenges. In tennis, this means being open to change, learning from every situation, and never becoming rigid in your approach. The more adaptable you are, the more resilient you become, able to thrive in any environment.

 Actionable Insight: In your next match, if your plan isn't working, pause and ask: "How can I adapt?" Try a new tactic, mindset, or routine, and reflect afterward on what you learned from being flexible.

June 5
THE VIRTUE OF FORTITUDE

> "You have inner strengths that enable you to bear up with difficulties of every kind. You have been given fortitude, courage, and patience. Why should I worry what happens if I am armed with the virtue of fortitude? Nothing can trouble or upset me."
>
> — Epictetus

Every tennis player faces moments of adversity — whether it's a string of lost points, a tough opponent, or a day when nothing seems to go right. Epictetus reminds us that fortitude is not just about enduring hardship, but about meeting it with calm strength and resolve. On the court, this means refusing to let frustration or setbacks shake your confidence. Instead, you draw on your inner resources — patience, courage, and resilience — to keep competing with focus and determination. Fortitude is what allows you to stay composed in a long, grueling match, to bounce back after mistakes, and to keep fighting for every point, no matter the score.

Actionable Insight: In your next match or practice, when you encounter a difficult moment, pause and remind yourself: "I have the strength to bear this." Notice how calling on your inner fortitude helps you reset, refocus, and play your best tennis — even in the face of adversity.

June 6
THE ENDURANCE OF THE PRESENT MOMENT

> "Don't let your reflection on the whole sweep of life crush you. Stay focused on the present situation and ask yourself why it's so unbearable and can't be survived."
> — MARCUS AURELIUS

When you're tired or discouraged, it's easy to become overwhelmed by the thought of what lies ahead — a long match, a tough season, a daunting opponent. The Stoics teach that endurance is found in the present moment. You don't need to survive the whole match at once; you only need to play the next point, take the next breath, make the next effort. By breaking challenges into manageable pieces and focusing on the now, you discover reserves of strength you didn't know you had.

Actionable Insight: During your next tough match or practice, when you feel overwhelmed, bring your focus back to just the next point or the next shot. Remind yourself: "I can survive this moment."

June 7
THE WISDOM OF ACCEPTANCE

> "Don't demand that things happen as you wish, but wish that they happen as they do, and your life will go smoothly."
> — Epictetus

Resistance to reality creates suffering. The Stoics teach that acceptance is a form of strength: the ability to embrace what is, rather than wasting energy wishing for something else. In tennis, this means accepting bad calls, tough draws, or your own mistakes as part of the journey. Acceptance doesn't mean giving up; it means starting from where you are, with clarity and resolve, and moving forward from there. This attitude makes you more resilient, less frustrated, and better able to respond constructively to whatever comes your way.

Actionable Insight: The next time you encounter something you don't like on court, pause and say: "This is what is. Now, what can I do?" Practice meeting reality with acceptance and action.

June 8
THE GRIT TO FINISH WHAT YOU START

> "Nothing great is created suddenly, any more than a bunch of grapes or a fig. If you tell me that you desire a fig, I answer you that there must be time. Let it first blossom, then bear fruit, then ripen."
>
> – Epictetus

Grit is the combination of passion and perseverance over the long haul. The Stoics remind us that all worthwhile achievements require time, effort, and the willingness to see things through. In tennis, this means sticking with your training plan, finishing every drill, and playing every match to the last point, even when the outcome seems certain. Grit is what carries you through the slow seasons, the hard losses, and the moments when motivation fades. It's the quiet determination to finish what you start, trusting that every effort, no matter how small, brings you closer to your goals.

 Actionable Insight: Choose one commitment — whether it's a training block, a tournament, or a tough match — and resolve to see it through to the end. When you're tempted to quit, remind yourself of the fruit that comes from patience and persistence.

June 9
THE RESILIENCE OF OPTIMISM

> "Very little is needed to make a happy life; it is all within yourself, in your way of thinking."
>
> — Marcus Aurelius

Optimism is not naive positivity, but the resilient belief that you can find meaning, growth, and even joy in every circumstance. The Stoics teach that happiness is an inside job, shaped by your thoughts and attitudes. In tennis, optimism helps you bounce back from setbacks, see opportunity in adversity, and maintain your motivation through tough times. It's the lens that turns challenges into adventures and losses into lessons.

 Actionable Insight: After your next setback, deliberately look for something positive — a lesson, a moment of progress, or an opportunity for growth. Practice framing every experience in a way that builds your optimism and resilience.

June 10
STRENGTH FORGED IN ADVERSITY

"Fire is the test of gold; adversity, of strong men."
— SENECA

Routine builds consistency, but it's adversity that reveals your strength. Just as fire purifies gold, challenges bring your true resilience to the surface. Every tough match, draining practice, or mental low point is a forge where your character is shaped. The Stoics taught that the wise don't avoid hardship — they welcome it as a crucible for growth. In tennis, that means seeing tough conditions, strong opponents, or mistakes not as threats, but as teachers. Your routine is the foundation, but it's your response to the unexpected that defines your mastery.

 Actionable Insight: Reflect on a recent challenge in your tennis journey. What did it reveal about your mindset or habits? Choose one aspect of your routine (mental or physical) to strengthen this week — something that will help you stay grounded the next time you're tested. Let your resilience be sharpened by the fire, not broken by it.

June 11
THE STRENGTH TO BEGIN AGAIN

> "Every new beginning comes from some other beginning's end."
>
> — Seneca

Resilience is not just about surviving what happens to you, but about having the courage to start over — again and again. In tennis, this means returning to the court after an injury, coming back from a losing streak, or simply resetting after a tough set. The Stoics remind us that every ending is also a new beginning, and that growth comes from embracing each fresh start with hope and determination. The willingness to begin again, without bitterness or regret, is a sign of true strength. It's how champions are made — not by never falling, but by always rising.

Actionable Insight: After a setback, loss, or break from tennis, set a small, clear goal for your return. Approach your next session or match as a new beginning, free from the weight of the past.

June 12
EMBRACE THE CLIMB

> "Do not pray for an easy life, pray for the strength to endure a difficult one."
>
> — Bruce Lee
> (Stoic-adjacent)

Improvement in tennis is rarely a smooth ascent. The Stoic mindset is not to wish for fewer obstacles, but to build the strength and resilience to overcome them. Whether it's a tough training block, a losing streak, or a persistent weakness in your game, see each challenge as an opportunity to develop grit and perseverance. The journey may be steep, but every step you take makes you stronger and more prepared for future tests.

 Actionable Insight: Identify one challenge you're currently facing in your tennis journey. Instead of avoiding it, commit to working through it this week — whether that means extra practice, seeking advice, or simply refusing to give up. Track your progress and celebrate your perseverance.

June 13
THE CALM WITHIN THE STORM

> "If you are distressed by anything external, the pain is not due to the thing itself, but to your estimate of it; and this you have the power to revoke at any moment."
> – Marcus Aurelius

Pressure is a constant in tennis — match points, tiebreaks, noisy crowds. The Stoics remind us that the real source of distress is not the situation, but our perception of it. You can choose to see pressure as a threat, or as an opportunity to test your skills and grow. The ability to find calm within the storm, to steady your mind and focus on the task at hand, is what separates the mentally tough from the rest.

Actionable Insight: In your next high-pressure moment, pause and take a deep breath. Tell yourself: "This is just another point. I choose how I see it." Notice how this shift in perception calms your nerves.

June 14
THE ENDURANCE OF HOPE

"Sometimes even to live is an act of courage."

— Seneca

There are days in tennis — and in life — when just showing up takes courage. When you're tired, discouraged, or doubting yourself, hope is the fuel that keeps you moving. The Stoics teach that endurance is not just about physical toughness, but about the inner resolve to keep going, even when the path is hard. Hope is not naive optimism; it's the stubborn belief that your effort matters, that things can improve, and that every day is a new chance to grow.

 Actionable Insight: On your hardest day this month, remind yourself: "Showing up is an act of courage." Celebrate your effort, no matter the outcome.

June 15
THE WISDOM OF LETTING GO

> "He who angers you conquers you."
>
> — Elizabeth Kenny
> (Stoic-adjacent)

Holding onto anger — over a bad call, a tough loss, or an opponent's behavior — only drains your energy and clouds your mind. The Stoics teach that letting go is an act of strength, not weakness. In tennis, the quicker you can release frustration, the faster you can return to clarity and resilience. Letting go is not about ignoring problems, but about refusing to be defined by them.

Actionable Insight: After your next frustrating moment, take three deep breaths and visualize letting your anger drift away. Refocus on the next point and the opportunity it brings.

June 16
THE ENDURANCE OF DAILY EFFORT

> "Well-being is attained by little and little, and nevertheless is no little thing itself."
>
> — Zeno

Big breakthroughs are built on small, daily efforts. The Stoics valued steady, incremental progress over dramatic leaps. In tennis, this means committing to your routines, showing up for every session, and trusting that each bit of effort adds up. Over time, these small acts of discipline create a foundation of resilience that carries you through the toughest challenges.

 Actionable Insight: Choose one small habit to practice every day this week — whether it's a footwork drill, a gratitude reflection, or a mental reset. Track your consistency and celebrate your progress.

June 17
THE RESILIENCE OF SELF-KNOWLEDGE

> "Know, first, who you are, and then adorn yourself accordingly."
>
> — Epictetus

Resilience begins with self-knowledge — the honest recognition of your strengths, weaknesses, triggers, and tendencies. The Stoics teach that when you know yourself, you can prepare for adversity, play to your strengths, and manage your weaknesses. In tennis, self-knowledge helps you set realistic goals, craft effective strategies, and recover from setbacks with wisdom.

Actionable Insight: After your next match, reflect on what you learned about yourself. What situations challenge you most? How can you use this knowledge to build greater resilience?

June 18
THE POWER OF REFLECTION

> "Let us examine our thoughts; let us examine our actions; let us examine our desires."
>
> — SENECA

Reflection is the engine of resilience. The Stoics practiced daily self-examination, learning from every experience. In tennis, regular reflection helps you identify patterns, correct mistakes, and reinforce positive habits. It's not about self-criticism, but about honest assessment and intentional improvement. The more you reflect, the more you learn — and the faster you grow.

Actionable Insight: Set aside ten minutes at the end of each week to review your tennis: What went well? What needs work? What did you learn about yourself? Use these insights to set goals for the week ahead.

June 19
THE ENDURANCE OF FAITH IN THE PROCESS

> "Patience is bitter, but its fruit is sweet."
>
> — Aristotle

Patience is often the hardest virtue to practice, especially when progress feels slow. The Stoics and their contemporaries remind us that the rewards of patience are worth the wait. In tennis, staying patient through long rallies, tough training blocks, and gradual improvement allows you to savor the sweet fruits of your labor when they finally arrive.

Actionable Insight: Pick one area of your game that's been slow to improve. Commit to a steady, patient practice routine, and measure your progress in small increments. When impatience arises, remind yourself that lasting success takes time.

June 20
THE STRENGTH TO ASK FOR HELP

> "No one is so courageous as not to be sometimes disconcerted."
>
> – Cicero
> (Stoic-adjacent)

Resilience doesn't mean going it alone. The Stoics recognized that even the strongest need support. In tennis, reaching out to a coach, a teammate, or a friend when you're struggling is a sign of wisdom, not weakness. Asking for help allows you to learn faster, recover more quickly, and build a network of support that sustains you through tough times.

Actionable Insight: If you're facing a challenge, ask someone you trust for advice or encouragement. Notice how this act of vulnerability strengthens your resilience.

June 21
THE ENDURANCE OF PURPOSE

> "He who has a why to live can bear almost any how."
> — Nietzsche
> (Stoic-influenced)

Purpose fuels resilience. The Stoics believed that knowing your "why" — your deepest reason for playing, competing, and striving — gives you the strength to endure any hardship. In tennis, your purpose might be the love of the game, the pursuit of mastery, or the desire to inspire others. When challenges arise, reconnect with your purpose and let it carry you through.

Actionable Insight: Write down your "why" for playing tennis. When you face adversity, read it to yourself and let it remind you of what makes your effort worthwhile.

June 22
THE WISDOM OF REST

> "Rest is not idleness, and to lie sometimes on the grass under trees on a summer's day, listening to the murmur of water, or watching the clouds float across the sky, is by no means a waste of time."
>
> — JOHN LUBBOCK
> (STOIC-ADJACENT)

Endurance is not just about pushing harder, but also about knowing when to rest. The Stoics valued balance and the wisdom to care for the body and mind. In tennis, rest is essential for recovery, growth, and long-term resilience. Taking time to recharge is not weakness, but a strategic investment in your future strength.

 Actionable Insight: Schedule a day of rest or active recovery this week. Use it to reflect, recharge, and return to the court with renewed energy.

June 23
THE RESILIENCE OF OPTIMISM

> "The bravest sight in the world is to see a great man struggling against adversity."
>
> — SENECA

Optimism is not simply expecting easy victories or smooth matches — it's the courageous belief that you can find meaning, growth, and even joy in the midst of struggle. Seneca reminds us that true bravery is revealed when someone faces adversity head-on, refusing to be broken by setbacks. In tennis, this means maintaining hope and determination even when you're down in the score, facing a tough opponent, or coming back from injury. The optimistic player doesn't deny difficulty; instead, they see struggle as a proving ground for their character and skills. By embracing adversity with a positive spirit, you inspire not only yourself but also those who watch you persevere. Each time you battle through a tough match or a challenging season, you're building the kind of resilience that lasts a lifetime — on and off the court.

Actionable Insight: After your next difficult session or loss, reflect on how you responded to adversity. Write down one way you showed courage in the face of struggle, and remind yourself that optimism is forged through these moments of challenge, not comfort.

June 24
TURN OBSTACLES INTO OPPORTUNITIES

> "Just as nature takes every obstacle, every impediment, and works around it — turns it to its purposes, incorporates it into itself — so, too, a rational being can turn each setback into raw material and use it to achieve its goal."
> — Marcus Aurelius

Every tennis player faces obstacles — whether it's a tough opponent, swirling wind, a bad line call, or an off day with your serve. Marcus Aurelius reminds us that these challenges aren't just hurdles to overcome; they are the very material from which your improvement is built. Imagine you're in a match and your opponent keeps attacking your backhand, or the wind keeps pushing your lobs long. Instead of getting frustrated, treat these situations as opportunities to adapt and refine your game. Use adversity to experiment with new tactics, strengthen your weaknesses, and build mental toughness.

 Actionable Insight: In your next practice or match, identify one obstacle you encounter — maybe it's a particular shot that's not working or a situation that rattles you.

June 25
THE STRENGTH TO FORGIVE YOURSELF

> "Do not be ashamed of mistakes and thus make them crimes."
>
> — CONFUCIUS
> (STOIC-ADJACENT)

Resilience includes the ability to forgive yourself for errors and move forward. The Stoics teach that mistakes are inevitable; what matters is how you respond. In tennis, self-forgiveness allows you to learn from losses without being weighed down by guilt or shame. It frees you to play the next point with a clear mind and a hopeful heart.

Actionable Insight: After your next mistake or loss, acknowledge it, extract the lesson, and then let it go. Say to yourself: "I forgive myself. I am learning and growing."

June 26
THE ENDURANCE OF JOY

> "Joy is not in things; it is in us."
>
> — Richard Wagner
> (Stoic-adjacent)

Joy is a powerful source of resilience. The Stoics remind us that true joy comes not from external achievements, but from the satisfaction of effort, growth, and connection. In tennis, playing with joy helps you weather tough times, bounce back from setbacks, and stay motivated for the long haul. Joy transforms endurance from a burden into a privilege.

 Actionable Insight: Before your next match or practice, recall what you love about tennis. Let that joy infuse your play, especially when things get tough.

June 27
THE RESILIENCE OF COMMUNITY

> "We are made for cooperation, like feet, like hands, like eyelids, like the rows of the upper and lower teeth."
> – MARCUS AURELIUS

Resilience is strengthened by connection. The Stoics believed that we are social beings, meant to support and uplift each other. In tennis, your teammates, coaches, and friends are sources of encouragement, perspective, and shared strength. Leaning on your community is not a sign of weakness, but a strategy for enduring and thriving together.

 Actionable Insight: Reach out to someone in your tennis circle this week — offer support, ask for advice, or simply share your journey. Notice how community strengthens your resilience.

June 28
THE POWER OF PERSPECTIVE

> "Man is not worried by real problems so much as by his imagined anxieties about real problems."
> — Epictetus

Perspective is a key to resilience. The Stoics teach that much of our suffering comes from our thoughts about events, not the events themselves. In tennis, anxiety about the outcome, fear of failure, or regret over past mistakes can be more draining than the actual challenges you face. By stepping back and seeing things in perspective, you can respond with calm and clarity, rather than being overwhelmed by imagined fears.

Actionable Insight: The next time you feel anxious or discouraged, pause and ask: "Is this problem as big as I'm making it? What would I say to a friend in this situation?" Use perspective to regain your balance.

June 29
THE ENDURANCE OF FAITH IN YOURSELF

> "You have within you right now, everything you need to deal with whatever the world can throw at you."
> — Brian Tracy (Stoic-adjacent)

Self-belief is the ultimate source of resilience. The Stoics remind us that you possess all the inner resources you need — courage, wisdom, patience, and strength. In tennis, believing in yourself allows you to keep fighting, to recover from setbacks, and to pursue your goals with passion. Faith in yourself is not arrogance, but the quiet confidence that you can handle whatever comes your way.

Actionable Insight: Before your next challenge, repeat to yourself: "I have what I need within me." Let this belief guide your actions and sustain your endurance.

June 30
THE TRIUMPH OF RESILIENCE

> "The greater the obstacle, the more glory in overcoming it."
> — Molière (Stoic-adjacent)

The Stoics saw life as a series of obstacles to be overcome, each one an opportunity for glory — not in the eyes of others, but in your own growth and self-mastery. In tennis, every hardship, every tough match, every comeback is a testament to your resilience. The triumph is not just in winning, but in enduring, adapting, and rising above each challenge. This is the true victory — the one that lasts long after the trophies have faded.

Actionable Insight: At the end of this month, reflect on the obstacles you faced and overcame. Celebrate your resilience, and set a new challenge for July, knowing that you have the strength to meet it.

June Wrap-Up

June has been a month of embracing growth through challenge and sustained effort. By facing obstacles head-on, adapting to setbacks, and committing to daily improvement, you've strengthened your resilience and deepened your love for the game. Carry this spirit forward — let every test refine your character and remind you that progress is built one determined step at a time, both on and off the court.

July Theme

Community, Friendship, and the Common Good — The Stoic Team Spirit

STOICISM IS NOT a solitary pursuit. The ancient Stoics saw each of us as a part of a greater whole, responsible not just for ourselves but for lifting up those around us. This month explores the Stoic commitment to community, friendship, and the common good — how these ideals elevate your tennis and your life.

July 1
THE STOIC HEART OF COMMUNITY

> "What brings no benefit to the hive brings none to the bee."
> — Marcus Aurelius

On the court, it's tempting to focus only on your own performance, your own goals, your own results. But Stoicism teaches that we are all part of a larger community — our team, our club, our tennis family. Just as a bee thrives only when the hive is healthy, your own growth and satisfaction are tied to the well-being of those around you. Supporting teammates, volunteering at events, cheering for others, and sharing your knowledge all strengthen the fabric of your community. When you give to the group, you also receive: motivation, camaraderie, and a sense of belonging that makes every victory sweeter and every setback lighter.

 Actionable Insight: This week, look for a way to contribute to your tennis community — help a teammate, organize a practice, or simply offer encouragement. Notice how this act of service uplifts both you and those around you.

July 2
THE VIRTUE OF FRIENDSHIP

> "Friendship produces between us a partnership in all our interests. There is no such thing as good or bad fortune for the individual; we live in common."
>
> — Seneca

Tennis is often seen as an individual sport, but the friendships you build are among its greatest rewards. The Stoics believed that friendship is a partnership — a sharing of fortunes, joys, and burdens. A true tennis friend is someone who celebrates your victories, supports you in defeat, and pushes you to grow. Friendship on the court is not just about having fun; it's about practicing kindness, loyalty, and honesty. By investing in these relationships, you not only enrich your own experience but also create a culture of trust and support that benefits everyone.

Actionable Insight: Reach out to a tennis friend today — thank them for their support, invite them to hit, or offer encouragement. Reflect on how your friendship helps you become a better player and person.

July 3
HELPING OTHERS AS A STOIC DUTY

"Man is born for deeds of kindness."

— Marcus Aurelius

The Stoics saw acts of kindness not as optional, but as our duty as human beings. In tennis, this means going out of your way to help others — whether it's offering advice to a beginner, picking up stray balls, or supporting a teammate through a slump. Kindness builds trust, strengthens bonds, and creates a positive environment where everyone can thrive. Remember, every small act of service contributes to the common good and reflects the best of Stoic virtue.

Actionable Insight: During your next session, find a small way to help someone else — without expecting anything in return. Notice how this simple act improves the atmosphere for everyone.

July 4
THE WISDOM OF COOPERATION

> "We were born to work together like feet, hands, and eyes, like the two rows of teeth, upper and lower."
> — Marcus Aurelius

Doubles, team matches, and even friendly rallies all require cooperation. The Stoics believed that humans are naturally designed to work together, each person contributing their unique strengths to the whole. On the court, this means communicating openly, sharing credit, and supporting your partner through mistakes and successes alike. When you see yourself as part of a team, you learn to celebrate others' victories as your own and to find joy in shared effort.

 Actionable Insight: In your next doubles or team match, focus on supporting your partner — offer encouragement, celebrate their good shots, and stay positive through errors. Reflect on how cooperation enhances your enjoyment and performance.

July 5
OPEN COMMUNICATION BUILDS TRUST

> "Foster open communication... The Stoics' emphasis on reason and clear thinking can be applied to encourage a culture where feedback is shared constructively, and dialogue is encouraged."
> – STOIC WISDOM FOR MODERN TEAM BUILDING

Trust and unity in any tennis community are built on honest, respectful communication. The Stoics valued reason and clarity, encouraging open dialogue and the constructive exchange of feedback. On the court, this means discussing tactics, sharing observations, and addressing conflicts calmly and directly. When communication is open, misunderstandings are resolved quickly, and everyone feels heard and valued.

Actionable Insight: This week, practice giving and receiving feedback with your team or doubles partner. Approach every conversation with curiosity and respect, aiming to build understanding and trust.

July 6
THE JOY OF SHARED SUCCESS

> "No one can live happily who has regard to himself alone and transforms everything into a question of his own utility; you must live for your neighbour, if you would live for yourself."
>
> — SENECA

While winning feels good, sharing success with others brings deeper joy. The Stoics remind us that fulfillment comes not from self-centered achievement, but from lifting others up and celebrating together. In tennis, this means rejoicing in your partner's improvement, your team's victories, and the growth of your community. When you focus on collective success, your own accomplishments become more meaningful and your setbacks easier to bear.

 Actionable Insight: After your next match or practice, take time to celebrate someone else's progress or success. Notice how sharing in their joy increases your own.

July 7
THE POWER OF EMPATHY

> "Cultivate empathy and understanding in our interpersonal relationships... listen to others in a way that acknowledges their own values, beliefs, and autonomy."
> – DAILY STOIC

Empathy is the ability to see the world through another's eyes. The Stoics believed that understanding others' perspectives builds stronger, more compassionate communities. On the court, empathy helps you support a struggling teammate, resolve conflicts peacefully, and learn from those different from yourself. Practicing empathy leads to deeper friendships, more effective teamwork, and a more harmonious tennis environment.

 Actionable Insight: The next time you disagree with someone on court, pause and try to see the situation from their perspective. Ask questions, listen deeply, and respond with understanding.

July 8
THE STRENGTH OF ACCOUNTABILITY

> "Cultivate self-discipline and personal accountability, recognizing that our reactions and emotions are within our control."
> — STOIC WISDOM FOR MODERN TEAM BUILDING

Teams and friendships flourish when each member takes responsibility for their actions and emotions. The Stoics taught that while we cannot control everything, we can always control our own conduct. On the court, this means owning your mistakes, apologizing when necessary, and striving to improve — not just for yourself, but for the good of the group. Accountability builds trust and sets a positive example for others.

Actionable Insight: After your next match, review your actions and reactions. If you made a mistake or lost your temper, own it and make amends. Notice how this strengthens your relationships and your own sense of integrity.

July 9
THE GIFT OF FRIENDSHIP

> "For what purpose, then, do I make a man my friend? In order to have someone for whom I may die, whom I may follow into exile, against whose death I may stake my own life, and pay the pledge, too."
>
> — SENECA

Stoic friendship is deep and loyal — a partnership in which you are willing to stand by your friend through thick and thin. On the tennis court, this means supporting your partner or teammate not just when things are easy, but especially when they are hard. True friendship is a source of strength, comfort, and inspiration. It's a place to practice kindness, honesty, and courage, knowing you have someone who will do the same for you.

 Actionable Insight: Reach out to a tennis friend who might be struggling or facing a challenge. Offer your support, listen without judgment, and remind them they are not alone.

July 10
THE COMMON GOOD AS THE HIGHEST GOAL

> "For all that I do, whether on my own or assisted by another, should be directed to this single end, the common benefit and harmony."
>
> — Marcus Aurelius

The Stoics believed that our highest purpose is to serve the common good. In tennis, this means putting the needs of the group above personal glory — helping organize events, welcoming new players, or stepping in to resolve conflicts. When you act for the benefit of all, you create a legacy of harmony and goodwill that endures far beyond any single match.

 Actionable Insight: This week, look for a way to serve your tennis community — volunteer, mediate, or simply offer a helping hand. Reflect on how this focus on the common good brings deeper satisfaction than any personal win.

July 11
THE VALUE OF TEACHING OTHERS

> "While we teach, we learn."
>
> — SENECA

One of the most powerful ways to deepen your own understanding and skill is to teach others. The Stoics recognized that sharing knowledge is not just an act of generosity, but also a profound opportunity for self-growth. On the tennis court, mentoring a less experienced player, explaining a drill, or simply offering encouragement forces you to clarify your own thinking and revisit fundamentals. Teaching also strengthens the bonds within your community, creating a culture where everyone lifts each other up. When you help others improve, you reinforce your own learning and contribute to the growth of the group as a whole.

Actionable Insight: This week, find an opportunity to teach or mentor someone in your tennis circle. Whether it's a tip, a drill, or a word of encouragement, notice how the act of teaching helps you reflect on and refine your own game.

July 12
HUMILITY IN VICTORY AND DEFEAT

"Receive without pride, let go without attachment."
— Marcus Aurelius

Whether you win or lose, the Stoic approach is to accept the outcome with humility and grace. Pride in victory can lead to arrogance, while attachment to winning can make losses unbearable. The true test of character is how you carry yourself regardless of the result. On the court, this means celebrating your wins without boasting, and accepting your losses without bitterness. By practicing humility, you maintain perspective, keep your relationships strong, and remain open to learning from every experience.

Actionable Insight: After your next match, regardless of the outcome, thank your opponent, congratulate others, and reflect on what you learned. Notice how humility brings peace and respect from those around you.

July 13
THE POWER OF SHARED GOALS

> "The whole is greater than the sum of its parts."
> — ARISTOTLE
> (STOIC-ADJACENT)

A team or community united by a common goal can achieve far more than any individual alone. The Stoics understood that when people come together with shared purpose — whether it's winning a league, building a club, or growing the game — each person's strengths amplify those of the group. In tennis, this means supporting team goals, celebrating collective achievements, and sacrificing personal glory for the good of all. Shared goals create unity, motivation, and a sense of belonging that enriches every aspect of your tennis journey.

Actionable Insight: At your next team practice or event, discuss a shared goal with your group. Commit to one action that will help the team, not just yourself, move closer to that goal.

July 14
THE IMPORTANCE OF GRATITUDE IN COMMUNITY

> "He is a wise man who does not grieve for the things which he has not, but rejoices for those which he has."
> — EPICTETUS

Gratitude is the glue that holds communities together. The Stoics teach us to focus on what we have, rather than what we lack. In tennis, this means appreciating your teammates, your coaches, your club, and the opportunity to play. Gratitude turns competition into celebration and rivalry into respect. When you express appreciation for those around you, you foster goodwill, deepen bonds, and create an atmosphere where everyone is motivated to give their best.

 Actionable Insight: This week, thank someone in your tennis community — a coach, partner, organizer, or even an opponent. Notice how gratitude strengthens your connection and lifts the spirit of the group.

July 15
THE STRENGTH OF DIVERSITY

> "We are more often frightened than hurt; and we suffer more from imagination than from reality."
>
> — SENECA

Diversity in a community — of playing styles, backgrounds, and perspectives — can be a source of strength rather than fear. The Stoics remind us that much of our anxiety comes from unfamiliarity, not from real danger. In tennis, embracing diversity means being open to learning from those who are different from you, whether it's a player with an unusual technique or a teammate from another culture. Diversity challenges your assumptions, expands your skills, and makes your community more resilient and creative.

 Actionable Insight: Connect with someone in your tennis circle who has a different background or style. Ask about their approach to the game, and see what new insights or techniques you can learn.

July 16
THE PRACTICE OF FORGIVENESS

> "Whenever you are about to find fault with someone, ask yourself the following question: What fault of mine most nearly resembles the one I am about to criticize?"
> — Marcus Aurelius

Conflict is inevitable in any group, but the Stoics teach that forgiveness is essential for lasting harmony. On the court, tempers may flare, mistakes may be made, and misunderstandings can arise. Practicing forgiveness — both towards others and yourself — frees you from resentment and keeps the community strong. By recognizing your own imperfections, you become more compassionate and patient with those around you.

 Actionable Insight: If you're holding a grudge against someone in your tennis circle, take a moment to reflect on your own fallibility. Reach out, offer forgiveness, or simply let go of the resentment for your own peace and the health of your community.

July 17
THE COURAGE TO SPEAK UP

> "If it is not right, do not do it; if it is not true, do not say it."
> – MARCUS AURELIUS

Communities thrive when members have the courage to speak up for what is right. The Stoics valued honesty and integrity, even when it was uncomfortable. On the court, this means calling your own lines fairly, addressing unsportsmanlike behavior, and standing up for teammates who need support. Speaking the truth, kindly but firmly, helps build a culture of respect and trust.

Actionable Insight: The next time you witness unfairness or dishonesty in your tennis environment, find a way to address it respectfully. Notice how your courage helps maintain the integrity of your community.

July 18
THE GENEROSITY OF SHARING SUCCESS

> "The wise man is content with his lot, whatever it may be, without wishing for what he has not."
>
> — Seneca

Success is sweetest when it's shared. The Stoics teach that contentment comes from appreciating what you have and sharing your good fortune with others. In tennis, this means celebrating not just your own victories, but also those of your teammates and rivals. Sharing success builds goodwill, motivates others, and creates a positive, uplifting environment for all.

 Actionable Insight: After your next win or accomplishment, share your happiness — whether by congratulating a teammate, posting a thank-you to your supporters, or simply inviting others to celebrate with you.

July 19
THE PATIENCE TO BUILD SOMETHING LASTING — TOGETHER

> "...we were born into this world to work together like the feet, hands, eyelids, or upper and lower rows of teeth."
> — MARCUS AURELIUS, MEDITATIONS 2.1

Building something meaningful in tennis — or in life — takes time, and it's rarely done alone. Marcus Aurelius reminds us that we are naturally designed for cooperation and community. Whether you're part of a doubles team, a practice group, or a supportive tennis club, your progress and enjoyment are amplified by the people around you. Shared drills, friendly matches, and even tough losses become opportunities to learn from and support each other. The patience to build lasting skills and relationships is strengthened when you invest in your tennis community, celebrate others' successes, and offer help or encouragement. When you work together, you create an environment where everyone grows stronger, both as players and as people.

Actionable Insight: This week, reach out to a teammate or practice partner — offer encouragement, share a tip, or simply thank them for being part of your tennis journey. Notice how supporting others not only builds community but also deepens your own sense of fulfillment and patience on the court.

July 20
THE JOY OF PLAYING FOR SOMETHING BIGGER

> "What you do for yourself dies with you; what you do for others remains and is immortal."
>
> — Marcus Aurelius

The Stoics believed that our highest fulfillment comes from serving others and contributing to something greater than ourselves. In tennis, playing for your team, your club, or your community gives every match deeper meaning. When you play for others, you find new reserves of motivation, resilience, and joy. Your efforts become part of a legacy that inspires and uplifts those who follow.

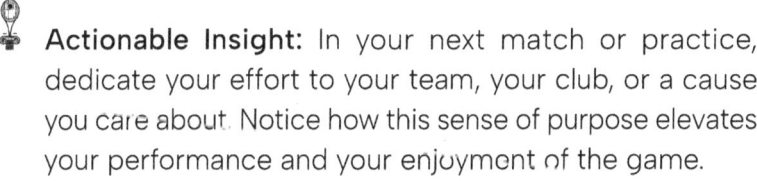 **Actionable Insight:** In your next match or practice, dedicate your effort to your team, your club, or a cause you care about. Notice how this sense of purpose elevates your performance and your enjoyment of the game.

July 21
THE WISDOM OF MUTUAL RESPECT

> "He who is not a good servant will not be a good master."
> — Plato (Stoic-adjacent)

Respecting others begins with respecting yourself and the role you play in a group. This quote reminds us that leadership and influence are earned through humility and service — not dominance. In tennis, mutual respect grows when each player is willing to listen, learn, and support their team or community with sincerity. Whether you're a captain or a casual player, when you serve others with good intent — by being punctual, positive, and coachable — you build trust and invite collaboration. Great teams and tennis environments thrive not on authority, but on earned respect through example.

 Actionable Insight: Think of one way you can serve your tennis group this week — showing up early, cleaning up after practice, or helping a teammate. Notice how small acts of service shift the group dynamic and elevate the respect shared among players.

July 22
THE GIFT OF HONEST FEEDBACK

"Let the wise man correct me, it is a kindness."
— SENECA

Constructive feedback is essential for growth, but it can be difficult to give and receive. The Stoics saw honest correction as an act of kindness, not criticism. In tennis, being open to feedback from coaches, teammates, and even opponents helps you see your blind spots and accelerate your improvement. Likewise, offering feedback with care and respect helps others grow and builds trust within your community.

Actionable Insight: Ask a teammate or coach for honest feedback on your game this week. Listen with an open mind, thank them, and apply what you learn. Offer thoughtful, supportive feedback to someone else in return.

July 23
THE STRENGTH OF SHARED STRUGGLE

> "I judge you unfortunate because you have never lived through misfortune. You have passed through life without an opponent — no one can ever know what you are capable of, not even you."
>
> — SENECA

In tennis, as in life, it's the battles — against tough opponents, grueling conditions, and your own limits — that reveal your true character. Seneca reminds us that struggle is not a curse, but a gift: without worthy opposition, you never discover your deepest strengths. The most memorable matches are not the easy wins, but the ones where you and your opponent push each other to new heights. Shared struggle on the court forges respect, camaraderie, and growth. When you face a challenging rival, you're both given the chance to find out what you're truly made of.

Actionable Insight: After your next tough match, take a moment to appreciate your opponent and the shared battle you endured. Reflect on how the struggle brought out your best, and consider reaching out to thank your rival for helping you grow as a competitor.

July 24
THE IMPORTANCE OF INCLUSION

"We are made for cooperation, like feet, like hands, like eyelids, like the rows of the upper and lower teeth."
— Marcus Aurelius

A strong tennis community is one where everyone feels welcome, regardless of skill, background, or experience. The Stoics believed that each person has a role to play in the greater whole. Inclusion means inviting new players, respecting differences, and valuing everyone's contribution. When you foster inclusion, you create a richer, more vibrant community where everyone can thrive and learn from one another.

Actionable Insight: At your next practice or event, introduce yourself to someone new or invite a less experienced player to join your group. Notice how inclusion strengthens your community and expands your own perspective.

July 25
THE POWER OF ENCOURAGEMENT

> "It is not that we have a short time to live, but that we waste much of it."
>
> — SENECA

Time on the court — and in life — is precious. The Stoics remind us not to waste opportunities to lift each other up. Encouragement is a simple but powerful way to make every moment count. Whether it's a high five, a supportive word, or a cheer from the sidelines, encouragement boosts confidence, motivation, and enjoyment for everyone involved.

 Actionable Insight: Make it a point to encourage at least three different people during your next tennis session. Notice how this positivity spreads and enhances the experience for all.

July 26
THE HUMILITY TO LEARN FROM ALL

> "If someone is able to show me that what I think or do is not right, I will happily change, for I seek the truth by which no one was ever truly harmed."
> — Marcus Aurelius

Humility is the willingness to learn from anyone — regardless of age, ranking, or experience. The Stoics valued truth and growth over ego. In tennis, this means being open to advice from a junior player, learning from an opponent's tactics, or accepting corrections from a coach. Every person you encounter has something to teach you, and every lesson learned makes your community stronger.

Actionable Insight: Ask someone you wouldn't normally seek advice from — a younger player, a new member, or even an opponent — what they see in your game. Approach their perspective with curiosity and gratitude.

July 27
THE JOY OF CELEBRATION

"Rejoice in the things that are present."
— Marcus Aurelius

Celebration is an important part of community life. The Stoics encourage us to find joy in the present moment and to share that joy with others. In tennis, this means celebrating not just victories, but effort, improvement, and the simple pleasure of playing together. Shared celebrations — team dinners, post-match rituals, or just a laugh after a long rally — build memories and strengthen bonds.

Actionable Insight: After your next match or practice, take time to celebrate with your group. Share what you enjoyed, acknowledge others' efforts, and savor the moment together.

July 28
THE SECURITY OF BELONGING

"He who is brave is free."

— SENECA

Belonging to a community gives you the courage to be yourself and to strive for more. The Stoics believed that true freedom comes from living in harmony with others, supported by mutual trust and respect. In tennis, knowing that you are valued and accepted by your team or club frees you to take risks, learn from mistakes, and pursue your goals without fear of judgment.

 Actionable Insight: Reflect on what makes you feel you belong in your tennis community. Reach out to someone who might feel left out and invite them to join in, strengthening the sense of security and freedom for all.

July 29
THE RESPONSIBILITY TO GIVE BACK

> "To whom much is given, much will be required."
>
> — SENECA
> (PARAPHRASED)

With experience and success comes the responsibility to give back. The Stoics teach that our gifts are not just for ourselves, but for the benefit of others. In tennis, this means mentoring newcomers, volunteering at events, or sharing your knowledge and passion with the next generation. Giving back enriches your own journey and ensures the health and growth of your community.

Actionable Insight: Identify one way you can give back to your tennis community this month — whether by coaching, organizing, or simply being a supportive presence. Take action and reflect on the impact you make.

July 30
THE ENDURING POWER OF LEGACY

> "What we do now echoes in eternity."
>
> — Marcus Aurelius

Your actions today shape the future of your community. The Stoics believed that our legacy is built not just on achievements, but on the values we embody and the lives we touch. In tennis, the way you treat others, the example you set, and the contributions you make will be remembered long after the scores are forgotten. Focus on building a legacy of kindness, integrity, and service that inspires those who follow.

 Actionable Insight: Reflect on the legacy you want to leave in your tennis community. What values do you want to be known for? Take one action today that aligns with this vision.

July 31
THE UNITY OF THE TEAM SPIRIT

> "We are waves of the same sea, leaves of the same tree, flowers of the same garden."
>
> — SENECA

At the heart of a Stoic community is the recognition that we are all connected. Every player, coach, and supporter is part of a larger whole, united by a love of the game and a commitment to each other's growth. When you embrace this unity, competition becomes collaboration, and every success is shared. The team spirit is not just about winning, but about belonging, supporting, and celebrating together.

Actionable Insight: At your next team event or practice, take a moment to acknowledge the unity of your group. Express gratitude for the connections you share and commit to strengthening the bonds that make your tennis community thrive.

July Wrap-Up: Playing with Integrity and Respect

As July comes to a close, we've explored how character — not just skill — defines your impact on the court. This month was about more than forehands and footwork. It was about **how you treat yourself, your opponents, and the game itself**. You've learned that true strength comes from humility, composure, honesty, and mutual respect.

Whether it was choosing encouragement over criticism, staying poised under pressure, or modeling sportsmanship when no one's watching, you've built a foundation for **ethical excellence**. These qualities don't just make you a better tennis player — they make you someone others trust, admire, and want to play with.

In the end, how you play matters just as much as how well you play. And when you align your game with your values, every match becomes an opportunity to lead by example.

August will bring new challenges, but your integrity will remain your most dependable weapon.

August Theme

Emotional Mastery — Stoic Calm in the Heat of Competition

Aᴜɢᴜsᴛ ᴇxᴘʟᴏʀᴇs ᴛʜᴇ Stoic art of emotional regulation — how to meet frustration, anger, and disappointment with composure, and how to cultivate joy and equanimity even in the most intense moments on court. This month, you'll learn to transform your emotional energy into focus, resilience, and lasting enjoyment of the game.

August 1
THE DISCIPLINE OF CALM

> "You have power over your mind — not outside events. Realize this, and you will find strength."
>
> — Marcus Aurelius

Tennis is an emotional sport. A single point can swing the momentum, and the pressure of competition can trigger frustration, anger, or anxiety. The Stoics remind us that while we cannot control every bounce or call, we always have the power to govern our own minds. When you learn to pause before reacting, to breathe through a surge of emotion, and to choose your response, you reclaim your strength. This inner discipline is what allows you to play your best tennis under pressure and to enjoy the game regardless of the outcome.

 Actionable Insight: During your next match, when you feel your emotions rising, pause and take three deep breaths. Remind yourself: "My mind is my domain." Notice how this simple act restores your focus and composure.

August 2
FRUSTRATION VS. ANGER — KNOW THE DIFFERENCE

> "Frustration is unhappiness about not playing well oneself. Anger is an emotion directed at either an opponent or one's doubles partner if she is judged to be making unforgivable errors."
>
> — WILLIAM O. STEPHENS

Understanding your emotions is the first step to mastering them. The Stoics teach that frustration often comes from falling short of your own standards, while anger is usually directed outward. On the court, frustration might arise from missing an easy shot; anger might flare when you believe an opponent made a bad call. Recognizing this difference allows you to address the root cause — improving your skills for frustration, practicing empathy and restraint for anger. Both emotions are natural, but neither should control your actions.

 Actionable Insight: After your next match, reflect on moments of frustration and anger. What triggered them? How did you respond? Make a plan for how you'll handle each emotion constructively next time.

August 3
THE FOLLY OF OUTBURSTS

> "All such outbursts are juvenile, unseemly, and unquestionably unsportsmanlike. Tantrums have no place on a tennis court or in any sport. Respect for your opponent (and doubles partner) always demands courtesy."
>
> – WILLIAM O. STEPHENS

Emotional outbursts — racket smashing, shouting, or cursing — do more than cost you points; they erode your focus, your reputation, and your relationships. The Stoics teach that self-control is a sign of maturity and wisdom. Losing your cool hands the advantage to your opponent and diminishes your enjoyment of the game. True strength is shown in how you handle adversity, not in how loudly you express your frustration.

 Actionable Insight: If you feel an outburst coming on, step back and count to ten. Channel your energy into the next point, and remember that your conduct is always under your control.

August 4
THE POWER OF COURTESY

"During a match adversity tests not only a player's tennis skills but even more her tenacity. Superior mental toughness and concentration often empower a player to prevail over a more skilled opponent with inferior mental focus."

— WILLIAM O. STEPHENS

Courtesy and respect for others are not just social niceties — they are competitive advantages. When you treat your opponent and officials with respect, you maintain your own mental clarity and composure. The Stoics saw every interaction as a chance to practice virtue. Even in the heat of battle, your ability to stay courteous and focused can tip the balance in your favor, especially against opponents who are less disciplined.

 Actionable Insight: Make it a point to thank your opponent and the officials after every match, win or lose. Notice how this habit enhances your reputation and your own sense of calm.

August 5
THE WISDOM OF PERSPECTIVE

> "Before making such a judgment Stoicism reminds us of our epistemic limitations."
>
> – WILLIAM O. STEPHENS

It's easy to assume the worst when you believe an opponent made a bad line call or a partner missed an easy shot. The Stoics caution us to remember our own limitations: we don't always see every angle or know every motive. Cultivating this humility helps you avoid unnecessary conflict and keeps your focus where it belongs — on your own game.

Actionable Insight: The next time you disagree on a call, pause and remind yourself: "I might not have seen it perfectly." Practice giving others the benefit of the doubt and move forward with grace.

August 6
ACCEPTANCE OF HONEST MISTAKES

> "People making honest mistakes do not deserve to be scolded. A pragmatic Stoic tennis player is epistemically cautious, and so is reluctant to attribute ill will to her opponent(s)."
>
> — William O. Stephens

Mistakes happen — by you, your partner, and your opponents. The Stoic approach is to accept honest errors as part of the game and of being human. Scolding or holding grudges over innocent mistakes only poisons your own mindset and the spirit of competition. By practicing acceptance and forgiveness, you keep your emotional energy available for positive action and learning.

Actionable Insight: When you or someone else makes a mistake, acknowledge it, forgive quickly, and refocus on the next point. Notice how this habit preserves your energy and enjoyment.

August 7
THE JOY OF PLAY

> "The point of playing any game is to have fun... If our play is not fun, then we are living contrary to the nature of play."
> — WILLIAM O. STEPHENS

It's easy to lose sight of joy when you're caught up in competition, striving for improvement, or dealing with setbacks. The Stoics remind us that tennis is, at its heart, a game — a form of play meant to be enjoyed. When you approach tennis with a sense of playfulness and gratitude, you tap into the original spirit of the sport. This joy not only makes you a better competitor but also sustains your motivation through ups and downs.

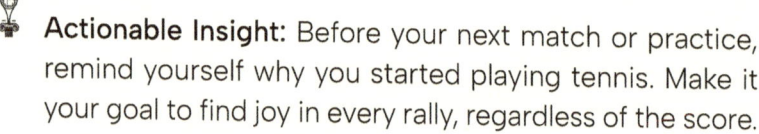 **Actionable Insight:** Before your next match or practice, remind yourself why you started playing tennis. Make it your goal to find joy in every rally, regardless of the score.

August 8
MASTERING THE SCORE

> "If someone loses track of the score, then the Stoic advice is to calmly consult with the other player(s), recall how each point went, and reconstruct the score."
>
> – William O. Stephens

Disputes over the score are common, but they need not become sources of conflict. The Stoic approach is to handle such situations with calm, reason, and good faith. By working together to reconstruct the score, you demonstrate respect for your opponent and for the game itself. This habit builds trust and keeps the focus on playing well, not on winning arguments.

 Actionable Insight: If there's a disagreement about the score, approach your opponent calmly and work together to recall each point. Practice patience and cooperation, knowing that the process matters more than the outcome.

August 9
THE ART OF LETTING GO

> "Pain is slight if opinion has added nothing to it; but if, on the other hand, you begin to encourage yourself and say, 'It is nothing, — a trifling matter at most; keep a stout heart and it will soon cease'; then in thinking it slight, you will make it slight."
>
> — SENECA

Dwelling on mistakes, bad calls, or missed opportunities only magnifies your suffering. The Stoics teach that much of our pain is created by our opinions and judgments, not by the events themselves. By learning to let go — seeing setbacks as small and temporary — you free yourself to move forward with confidence and clarity.

 Actionable Insight: After a tough point or call, repeat to yourself: "It is nothing — a trifling matter at most." Practice moving on quickly, and notice how your resilience grows.

August 10
TURNING EMOTION INTO FOCUS

> "Every difficulty in life presents us with an opportunity to turn inward and to invoke our own submerged inner resources. The trials we endure can and should introduce us to our strengths."
>
> — SENECA

Strong emotions are not your enemy; they are signals that you care. The Stoics teach us to use these emotions as fuel for focus and self-discovery. When you face adversity on the court, turn inward — find your breath, your resolve, your strategy. Every challenge is a chance to discover new strengths and deepen your mastery of the game and yourself.

 Actionable Insight: The next time you feel overwhelmed by emotion during a match, pause and ask: "What strength can I draw on right now?" Use your feelings as a signal to focus and play your best.

August 11
THE WISDOM OF EMOTIONAL DETACHMENT

> "Do not anticipate trouble, or worry about what may never happen. Keep in the sunlight."
> — BENJAMIN FRANKLIN (STOIC-ADJACENT)

Worrying about what might go wrong in a match — double faults, bad calls, or tough opponents — only distracts you from what's happening now. Emotional detachment is the art of letting go of imagined troubles and choosing to play in the "sunlight" of the present moment. When you focus on the point at hand, you play with more freedom and less anxiety.

Actionable Insight: If you catch yourself worrying about the future during a match, say to yourself: "Keep in the sunlight." Bring your attention back to your breath and the ball.

August 12
THE POWER OF SELF-COMPASSION

> "To bear trials with a calm mind robs misfortune of its strength and burden."
>
> — SENECA

Self-compassion is not about making excuses, but about meeting your mistakes and setbacks with a calm, constructive mind. When you treat yourself with the same patience you'd offer a friend, you rob misfortune of its power to discourage you. This allows you to recover faster from errors and approach each new point with renewed clarity and resolve.

Actionable Insight: After a tough point or match, pause and ask: "How would I encourage a friend right now?" Offer yourself the same calm support, then move forward.

August 13
THE FUTILITY OF COMPLAINING

> "If you are irritated by every rub, how will your mirror be polished?"
>
> — Rumi (Stoic-adjacent)

Every annoyance — bad bounces, noisy crowds, tough opponents — is a chance to polish your character. Complaining only dulls your focus and clouds your mind. The Stoic approach is to use each "rub" as an opportunity to grow more patient, adaptable, and resilient.

Actionable Insight: When you feel the urge to complain, pause and ask: "How can this moment polish my game?" Refocus on what you can do, not what you wish were different.

August 14
EMOTIONAL RESILIENCE THROUGH PREPARATION

> "To bear trials with a calm mind robs misfortune of its strength and burden."
>
> — SENECA

Emotional resilience is not about avoiding adversity, but about preparing your mind to respond with calm and clarity when it arrives. The Stoics teach that a steady mind, built through preparation and self-awareness, can withstand even the toughest challenges. In tennis, this means using your practice not just for physical skills, but for mental rehearsal — visualizing setbacks, pressure points, and unexpected events, and seeing yourself respond with composure. When you've trained yourself to remain calm, you're less likely to be thrown off by nerves or surprises. True preparation is as much about your mind as your body, and it's this inner calm that lets you play your best under stress.

Actionable Insight: Before your next match, spend five minutes visualizing difficult scenarios — bad calls, tough opponents, or momentum swings. Picture yourself responding with deep breaths and focused routines. After the match, reflect on how this mental preparation helped you remain steady when adversity struck.

August 15
THE STRENGTH OF RESTRAINT

> "He who conquers himself is the mightiest warrior."
> — CONFUCIUS (STOIC-ADJACENT)

The greatest battles in tennis are not against opponents, but within yourself — against impatience, frustration, or the urge to give up. Restraint is the ability to pause, to choose your response, and to act with wisdom rather than impulse. Each time you master your reactions, you become stronger, more consistent, and more respected — by others and by yourself.

Actionable Insight: Identify one recurring impulse that trips you up on court. This week, each time it arises, pause and remind yourself: "I am the mightiest warrior when I conquer myself."

August 16
THE VALUE OF EMOTIONAL HONESTY

> "The greatest griefs are those we cause ourselves."
> — Sophocles (Stoic-adjacent)

It's tempting to blame losses or frustration on opponents, conditions, or luck. But the Stoics teach that much of our suffering comes from our own judgments and stories. Emotional honesty means recognizing how your thoughts shape your feelings, and taking responsibility for your reactions. On the court, this awareness is the first step toward real change and growth.

Actionable Insight: After a match, reflect on a strong emotion you felt. Ask: "How did my own thoughts or expectations contribute to this feeling?" Use that insight to adjust your mindset next time.

August 17
THE PRACTICE OF EQUANIMITY

> "Nothing, to my way of thinking, is a better proof of a well-ordered mind than a man's ability to stop just where he is and pass some time in his own company."
>
> — SENECA

Equanimity is the ability to remain steady and composed, regardless of what's happening around you. The Stoics saw this as a sign of a well-ordered mind — one that can pause, reflect, and reset in the midst of chaos. In tennis, this means not being swept away by the highs and lows, but returning to your center and playing each point with calm focus.

Actionable Insight: During your next match, when momentum swings, use changeovers to pause, breathe, and recenter yourself. Practice being your own anchor, no matter the score.

August 18
THE WISDOM OF LEARNING FROM EMOTION

> "The mind that is anxious about future events is miserable."
> — Seneca

Emotions like anxiety, fear, or anger are not signs of weakness but invitations to learn. The Stoics teach that much of our misery comes from worrying about what might happen, rather than facing what is. In tennis, use your emotions as cues to return to the present, to learn what triggers you, and to practice responding with wisdom.

 Actionable Insight: After a match, write down one emotion that distracted you. What future event were you anxious about? How can you bring your focus back to the present next time?

August 19
THE POWER OF EMOTIONAL CONTAGION

> "Associate with people who are likely to improve you."
> — Seneca

Emotions are contagious — your calm can settle a team, your anxiety can spread, your joy can lift the whole court. The Stoics advise surrounding yourself with those who inspire and elevate you. In tennis, seek out partners and friends who model emotional mastery, and strive to be that person for others. Together, you create an environment where everyone can thrive.

Actionable Insight: Notice the emotional tone of your next practice or match. Are you contributing positivity and calm? Seek out those who inspire you, and be intentional about the energy you bring.

August 20
THE LIBERATION OF LETTING GO

> "It is not death that a man should fear, but he should fear never beginning to live."
>
> – Marcus Aurelius

Letting go of anger or resentment is not about ignoring injustice, but about refusing to let it control your life. The Stoics teach that clinging to negative emotions keeps you from fully engaging with the present and living your best life. On court, letting go frees you to play with joy and courage, unburdened by the past.

Actionable Insight: If anger or frustration lingers after a match, ask yourself: "What am I missing by holding onto this?" Choose to let go and embrace the next opportunity to play and live fully.

August 21
THE STRENGTH OF REFLECTION

> "To make mistakes is human; to profit by them is divine."
> – Elbert Hubbard (Stoic-adjacent)

Daily reflection is not about dwelling on errors, but about learning from them. The Stoics believed that reviewing your actions and emotions each day is the path to wisdom. In tennis, honest reflection transforms mistakes into lessons and setbacks into stepping stones for growth.

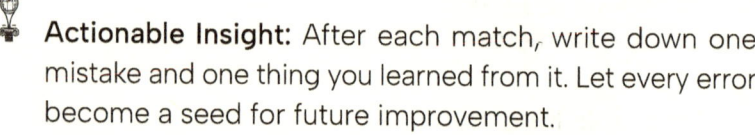 **Actionable Insight:** After each match, write down one mistake and one thing you learned from it. Let every error become a seed for future improvement.

August 22
THE POWER OF POSITIVE RITUALS

"Nothing happens to any man that he is not formed by nature to bear."

— Marcus Aurelius

Rituals help you face whatever comes, reminding you that you are equipped to handle any challenge. The Stoics teach that you are naturally capable of bearing the pressures and surprises of competition. In tennis, positive rituals — like a pre-point routine or a post-match review — anchor you in the present and reinforce your resilience.

Actionable Insight: Choose or refine a ritual that helps you reset during matches. Use it as a reminder: "I am formed to bear whatever comes."

August 23
THE JOY OF EMOTIONAL FREEDOM

> "There is nothing good or bad, but thinking makes it so."
> — SHAKESPEARE (STOIC-ADJACENT)

Your experience on court is shaped not by events themselves, but by how you interpret them. The Stoics teach that emotional freedom comes from choosing thoughts that serve you — focusing on opportunity rather than loss, on gratitude rather than frustration. This mindset allows you to play with joy, regardless of circumstances.

Actionable Insight: When a negative thought arises during play, pause and ask: "Is there another way to see this?" Practice reframing your experience in a positive light.

August 24
THE COURAGE TO FEEL

> "Begin at once to live, and count each separate day as a separate life."
>
> — SENECA

Courage on the court is not just about charging the net or playing through injury — it's about allowing yourself to fully show up, emotionally and mentally, in each moment. The Stoics taught that life should be lived as if each day were its own contained existence. In tennis, that means releasing the baggage of the past point and not overthinking the consequences of the next one. When you treat each point like a clean slate, you give yourself permission to play boldly, without fear or regret. Feeling nerves, disappointment, or hope is not a weakness — it's proof you're alive, engaged, and committed. Don't hold back. Let those emotions energize you.

 Actionable Insight: Before your next match, remind yourself: "This point is its own life." Use each serve and rally as a chance to reset, compete, and feel fully present — no matter what just happened or what's ahead.

August 25
THE WISDOM OF NOT TAKING THINGS PERSONALLY

> "It is not things themselves that disturb us, but our opinions about them."
>
> — Epictetus

When you take things personally — an opponent's celebration, a coach's critique — you give away your power. The Stoics remind us that it's our opinions, not the events themselves, that cause distress. By choosing a more helpful interpretation, you protect your peace and keep your focus on your own growth.

Actionable Insight: The next time you feel slighted, pause and ask: "What story am I telling myself?" Choose a narrative that keeps you empowered and focused.

August 26
THE PRACTICE OF EMOTIONAL GENEROSITY

> "Kindness is invincible, but only when it's sincere, with no hypocrisy or faking."
>
> — Marcus Aurelius

Genuine kindness on court — whether in victory or defeat — has the power to transform the emotional climate for everyone. The Stoics teach that sincere kindness is a strength, not a weakness. When you offer encouragement or a friendly gesture, you not only uplift others but also reinforce your own emotional mastery.

 Actionable Insight: Find a moment in your next match to offer a sincere word of encouragement or a gesture of sportsmanship. Notice how it affects your own mood and the atmosphere around you.

August 27
THE LIBERATION OF ACCEPTANCE

> "Accept whatever comes to you woven in the pattern of your destiny, for what could more aptly fit your needs?"
> – Marcus Aurelius

Acceptance is not resignation, but the wisdom to meet each moment as it comes. The Stoics teach that when you accept what is woven into your experience, you gain the freedom to respond with creativity and strength. In tennis, this means embracing the match you have, not the one you wish for, and making the most of every opportunity.

Actionable Insight: If you're frustrated by something out of your control, pause and say: "This is woven into my story today. How can I use it?" Let acceptance open the door to new possibilities.

August 28
THE STRENGTH OF EMOTIONAL CONSISTENCY

"A gem cannot be polished without friction, nor a man perfected without trials."

— Seneca

Consistency in your emotional responses is forged through repeated trials. The Stoics teach that challenges are what polish your character. In tennis, every tough match, every emotional test, is an opportunity to become more steady, more resilient, and more masterful.

 Actionable Insight: After a challenging match, reflect on how you handled emotional ups and downs. Celebrate your progress, and set a goal for even greater consistency next time.

August 29
THE VALUE OF EMOTIONAL REFLECTION

> "The unexamined life is not worth living."
> — Socrates (Stoic-adjacent)

Reflection is essential for emotional mastery. The Stoics teach that examining your thoughts, actions, and feelings leads to wisdom and growth. In tennis, regular reflection helps you understand your triggers, your strengths, and your opportunities for improvement.

 Actionable Insight: After each match, spend a few minutes journaling about your emotional experience. What did you learn? What will you try differently next time?

August 30
THE JOY OF EMOTIONAL MASTERY

"He who laughs at himself never runs out of things to laugh at."

— Epictetus (Stoic-adjacent)

Emotional mastery includes the ability to find humor and lightness, even in adversity. The Stoics valued the freedom that comes from not taking yourself too seriously. In tennis, being able to laugh at your mistakes, to smile after a tough point, and to enjoy the game regardless of the outcome is a sign of true mastery.

 Actionable Insight: The next time you make a mistake or feel pressure, try smiling or even laughing at yourself. Notice how this shifts your emotional state and brings joy back to the game.

August 31
THE ONGOING JOURNEY

"As long as you live, keep learning how to live."

— Seneca

Emotional mastery is a lifelong journey. The Stoics remind us that every day is a new opportunity to learn, to grow, and to deepen our understanding of ourselves. In tennis, each match, each practice, each emotional challenge is a lesson in living more fully and playing more freely.

Actionable Insight: At the end of this month, reflect on what you've learned about your emotions and yourself. Set an intention to keep learning, both on and off the court, every day.

Stoic Tennis

In August, you faced the true battleground of tennis: your emotions. You explored what it means to stay grounded when the score tightens, to breathe through frustration, and to compete with clarity in the face of pressure. Emotional mastery, the Stoics remind us, isn't the absence of feeling — it's the ability to act with reason even when your emotions roar.

Tennis constantly tests this skill. A bad call, a double fault at break point, or an opponent's mind games can derail a player who hasn't trained their inner world. But the composed player — the one who resets quickly, who doesn't chase the past or fear the future — holds the real advantage. Stoic calm is not passive stillness; it's **deliberate poise under fire**.

You've learned to recognize the first flicker of anger before it flares, to channel nervous energy into focused footwork, and to respond — not react — when matches grow tense. In doing so, you've started to develop what every great competitor possesses: the ability to stay composed while others unravel.

This month reminded you that tennis is not just physical or tactical — it's emotional chess. And the player who stays centered, who **lets go of what they cannot control and sharpens what they can**, will always be dangerous.

Take these lessons forward. Let calm become your competitive edge, and let clarity — not emotion — drive your next shot.

September Theme

The Virtue of Curiosity — Lifelong Learning On and Off the Court

SEPTEMBER IS DEDICATED to curiosity — the Stoic drive to keep learning, questioning, and growing, no matter your age or level. The greatest players and thinkers never stop asking "Why?" or "How can I improve?" Curiosity transforms setbacks into lessons and routines into experiments. This month, you'll use the Stoic spirit of inquiry to unlock new possibilities in your tennis and your mindset.

September 1
EMBRACE THE BEGINNER'S MIND

> "Every new beginning comes from some other beginning's end."
>
> — SENECA

No matter how experienced you are, there's always something more to learn. The Stoics valued humility and the willingness to start fresh, seeing each day as a new opportunity for growth. In tennis, approaching each practice or match with a beginner's mind lets you see old skills in a new light and stay open to unexpected insights. Curiosity keeps your game evolving and your motivation high. By letting go of the need to always be the expert, you free yourself to experiment, adapt, and discover new strengths. This mindset not only prevents stagnation but also rekindles your passion for the game, making every session an adventure in learning.

Actionable Insight: In your next session, pick one basic skill — like your grip or footwork — and approach it as if you're learning it for the first time. Ask questions, watch others, and experiment. Notice what fresh perspective you gain, and write down one new thing you discovered about your game.

September 2
ASK BETTER QUESTIONS

> "Nature gave us one tongue and two ears so we could listen more and talk less." — Epictetus

TENNIS INTERPRETATION:

Curiosity isn't just about seeking answers — it's about asking the right questions and truly listening. In tennis, this means being attentive to your coach, your body, and your results. The more you listen and inquire, the more you uncover subtle details that can elevate your game. Listening with intention allows you to pick up on feedback you might otherwise miss, and asking thoughtful questions can unlock breakthroughs in your technique or strategy. The Stoics believed that wisdom begins with listening, and in tennis, this practice can help you become more coachable and adaptable, leading to continuous improvement.

 Actionable Insight: After your next practice, ask your coach or a peer for one thing they notice about your play. Listen without defending or explaining. Write down their feedback and one follow-up question for next time. Reflect on how this new information can be applied to your next session.

September 3
LEARN FROM EVERY OPPONENT

> "Wise men learn more from fools than fools from the wise."
> — Cato the Elder (Stoic-adjacent)

Every opponent, strong or weak, has something to teach you. The Stoics believed you could learn from anyone if you're humble and curious. Instead of seeing matches only as tests of skill, treat them as opportunities to observe, adapt, and grow — especially when things don't go as planned. Even a loss can be a valuable lesson if you approach it with the right mindset. By analyzing your opponent's tactics and your own reactions, you gain insights that can be applied in future matches. This approach turns every competition, regardless of the outcome, into a stepping stone for personal growth and mastery.

Actionable Insight: After your next match, list three things your opponent did that challenged you. Reflect on how you might incorporate or counter those tactics in your own game. Make a plan to experiment with one of these ideas in your next practice.

September 4
CURIOSITY OVER EGO

"The first and greatest victory is to conquer yourself."
— Zeno of Citium

Ego resists feedback and avoids mistakes. Curiosity welcomes both as fuel for growth. The Stoics taught that true strength comes from self-mastery and the willingness to question your habits. In tennis, let curiosity, not pride, guide your improvement — especially when you're struggling. When you drop your guard and admit you don't know everything, you open yourself to new techniques, strategies, and ways of thinking. This humility allows you to turn setbacks into opportunities for learning, and keeps your progress from stalling. Over time, curiosity transforms your weaknesses into strengths and your frustrations into breakthroughs.

 Actionable Insight: Identify one area where you tend to get defensive (e.g., after a loss or critique). This week, approach it with curiosity: What can I learn here? How could I see this differently? Take notes on what you discover, and discuss your findings with a coach or teammate.

September 5
THE JOY OF EXPERIMENTATION

> "Nothing great is created in anger or haste."
>
> — Seneca

Curiosity thrives in a calm, open mind. When you experiment with new tactics, routines, or mindsets, you're more likely to discover breakthroughs. The Stoics remind us that impatience and frustration stifle creativity — whereas curiosity opens doors. Tennis is a sport that rewards those who are willing to try, fail, and try again, learning from each attempt. By viewing each practice as a laboratory for experimentation, you take the pressure off yourself to be perfect and instead focus on growth. This playful approach not only enhances your skills but also makes training more enjoyable and sustainable in the long run.

 Actionable Insight: Try one new tactic or routine in your next practice — whether it's a different warm-up, a new serve placement, or a mental cue. Observe the results without judgment and adjust as needed. At the end of your session, jot down what worked, what didn't, and how you felt during the process.

September 6
THE COURAGE TO ASK "WHY?"

> "Nothing is more surprising than the easiness with which the many are governed by the few."
> — SENECA

Curiosity means not taking things at face value — questioning routines, strategies, and even your own habits. The Stoics remind us that much of what we accept as "how things are" is simply convention, not necessity. In tennis, asking "Why do I do it this way?" can uncover areas where you're following old patterns that no longer serve you. This willingness to challenge assumptions is the spark for innovation and growth. By examining your routines and beliefs, you open the door to breakthroughs that others miss, staying ahead of the curve and keeping your game fresh.

 Actionable Insight: Pick one aspect of your training or match routine that you've never questioned. Ask yourself "Why do I do it this way?" Research or discuss alternatives with a coach, and try a small adjustment. Notice if this change brings new energy or effectiveness to your game.

September 7
FIND LESSONS IN THE ORDINARY

> "Observe constantly that all things take place by change."
> — Marcus Aurelius

Curiosity isn't just for dramatic moments — it thrives in the ordinary. The Stoics teach us that change is the only constant, and every day brings subtle shifts in your game, your body, and your mind. By observing these small changes, you become more attuned to your development. In tennis, this means noticing how your forehand feels today versus last week, or how your mindset shifts during a long rally. These observations, though small, can reveal patterns and opportunities for improvement that are invisible to the inattentive player.

 Actionable Insight: During your next practice, pay close attention to a single stroke or movement. Jot down how it feels, what's different from yesterday, and what you notice about your body or thoughts. Over time, use these notes to track your evolution and spot trends you might otherwise miss.

September 8
CURIOSITY AS A SOURCE OF MOTIVATION

"He who is brave is free."

— SENECA

Curiosity and courage go hand in hand. The Stoics believed that the brave are free because they are not afraid to explore, to ask, or to fail. In tennis, approaching each session with curiosity transforms fear of mistakes into excitement for discovery. When you're motivated by the question "What can I learn today?" rather than "Will I win?" you play with more freedom and less anxiety. This mindset keeps you energized, even through setbacks, and helps you bounce back quickly from frustration.

 Actionable Insight: Set a curiosity-based goal for your next match or practice, such as "I want to discover one new thing about my backhand." Let this goal guide your focus and keep you motivated, regardless of the score.

September 9
THE WISDOM OF NOT KNOWING

> "It is impossible for a man to learn what he thinks he already knows."
>
> — Epictetus

Admitting you don't know everything is the first step to real growth. The Stoics valued the humility of the perpetual student, always open to new knowledge. In tennis, this means letting go of the need to be right or to appear skilled, and instead embracing the unknown. When you approach lessons, matches, and even losses with the mindset of "What don't I know yet?" you accelerate your development and avoid the trap of stagnation.

 Actionable Insight: After your next match or lesson, write down three things you realized you don't fully understand about your game. Make a plan to investigate or ask about one of them this week.

September 10
LEARN FROM NATURE'S RHYTHM

"Nature does not hurry, yet everything is accomplished."
— Lao Tzu (Stoic-adjacent)

Curiosity is about observing, not forcing. The Stoics and their contemporaries saw nature as the ultimate teacher — progress happens in cycles, not in straight lines. In tennis, your growth will have ups and downs, bursts of insight, and periods of plateau. By studying these rhythms with curiosity rather than frustration, you learn to trust the process and work with your natural pace of improvement. This patience allows you to absorb lessons more deeply and avoid burnout.

Actionable Insight: Reflect on your last month of training. Where did you see unexpected progress? Where did you plateau? Accept these rhythms as natural and use curioslty, not judgment, to guide your next steps.

September 11
CURIOSITY FUELS ADAPTATION

> "Nothing is stable in human affairs, avoid undue elation in prosperity, or undue depression in adversity."
>
> — SOCRATES

Curiosity is the antidote to complacency. The Stoics and their philosophical kin teach us that nothing in life — or in tennis — remains the same for long. Your skills, your mindset, and your circumstances are always evolving. By staying curious, you become more adaptable, ready to adjust your strategy or mindset as needed. Instead of clinging to what worked yesterday, you approach each match as a fresh puzzle to solve. This openness not only helps you handle setbacks with resilience but also lets you spot new opportunities for growth that others might miss. Curiosity transforms adversity into a chance to learn, keeping you engaged and motivated no matter the outcome.

Actionable Insight: After your next match, review one moment when things didn't go as expected. Ask yourself, "What changed, and how could I have adapted?" Write down one new adjustment to try next time.

September 12
THE VALUE OF WONDER

"Wonder is the beginning of wisdom."
— Socrates

Every great discovery starts with a sense of wonder. The Stoics valued the ability to marvel at the world, seeing each experience as a chance to learn something new. On the tennis court, this means approaching your training and matches with a sense of awe and curiosity, even about the basics. When you allow yourself to be amazed by the complexity of a perfect rally or the subtlety of a spin serve, you open your mind to deeper learning. Wonder keeps your passion alive and helps you break through plateaus by inspiring you to look closer and experiment more.

 Actionable Insight: During your next practice, pick one aspect of the game — like the bounce of the ball or your footwork — and observe it with fresh eyes. See if you can notice something you've never paid attention to before. Let that sense of wonder guide your focus.

September 13
CURIOSITY OVERCOMES FEAR

> "Do not be afraid to give up the good to go for the great."
> — JOHN D. ROCKEFELLER (STOIC-ADJACENT)

Fear can keep you clinging to what's comfortable, but curiosity encourages you to reach higher. The Stoics teach that growth requires letting go of certainty and embracing the unknown. In tennis, this might mean trying a new grip, entering a tougher tournament, or learning a new style of play. While fear whispers that you might fail, curiosity asks, "What if I succeed?" By focusing on what you can discover — rather than what you might lose — you unlock new levels of performance and satisfaction. Curiosity gives you the courage to experiment and the resilience to bounce back from setbacks.

 Actionable Insight: Identify one area of your game where you've been playing it safe. This week, take one small risk — try a new tactic, shot, or routine. Reflect afterward on what you learned, regardless of the result.

September 14
THE POWER OF OPEN-MINDEDNESS

"Strong minds discuss ideas, average minds discuss events, weak minds discuss people."

— SOCRATES

Open-mindedness is a hallmark of the curious athlete. The Stoics believed in focusing on ideas and principles rather than gossip or complaints. In tennis, this means seeking out new perspectives, learning from different coaching styles, and being receptive to unconventional advice. By keeping your mind open, you expand your toolkit and become a more versatile competitor. This willingness to consider new ideas can help you break through plateaus and adapt to any opponent or situation.

 Actionable Insight: Ask a teammate or coach for an unconventional tip or drill. Try it out in your next practice, even if it feels odd at first. Reflect on how being open-minded can reveal new strengths or insights.

September 15
THE GIFT OF LIFELONG LEARNING

> "As long as you live, keep learning how to live."
> — SENECA

The Stoics saw life as a continuous journey of learning. No matter your age or experience, there is always more to discover — about tennis, about yourself, and about the world. Lifelong learning keeps your mind sharp and your game evolving. In tennis, this means staying curious about new techniques, strategies, and even your own habits. It's never too late to improve, and every day on the court is a new opportunity to grow. By embracing the mindset of a lifelong learner, you ensure that your passion for tennis — and for life — never fades.

Actionable Insight: Sign up for a clinic, watch a tutorial, or read an article about an aspect of tennis you've never explored. Commit to learning one new thing this week and applying it in your practice.

September 16
CURIOSITY UNLOCKS GROWTH

> "Nothing, to my way of thinking, is better proof of a well-ordered mind than a man's ability to stop just where he is and pass some time in his own company."
>
> — SENECA

Curiosity isn't just about seeking new skills; it's also about pausing to reflect on what you've learned and how you're growing. The Stoics valued the ability to look inward and examine one's own progress. In tennis, taking time to honestly assess your game — without judgment — opens the door to meaningful improvement. When you're willing to ask yourself what's working and what isn't, you become your own best coach. This habit of self-inquiry transforms plateaus into launching pads for new breakthroughs, and ensures you're always moving forward, no matter how small the step.

Actionable Insight: After your next practice, spend five quiet minutes reflecting on your session. What did you learn? What surprised you? Write down one question you want to explore in your next practice.

September 17
THE ADVENTURE OF TRYING NEW THINGS

> "It is not because things are difficult that we do not dare; it is because we do not dare that things are difficult."
> — SENECA

Curiosity invites you to try what you've never tried before. The Stoics remind us that fear of the unknown often makes improvement seem harder than it is. In tennis, daring to attempt a new tactic, shot, or routine — even if you might fail at first — can lead to unexpected progress. By embracing experimentation, you keep your training fresh and your mind engaged. Every new challenge faced with curiosity is an adventure that expands your skills and your confidence.

Actionable Insight: This week, pick one shot, tactic, or routine you've hesitated to try. Work it into your practice, even if it feels awkward. Reflect on what you learned from the experience, regardless of the outcome.

September 18
CURIOSITY AND RESILIENCE

"Difficulties strengthen the mind, as labor does the body."
— Seneca

Curiosity doesn't shy away from setbacks — it seeks to understand them. The Stoics believed that challenges are the best teachers, and that a curious mind is resilient in the face of adversity. In tennis, when you encounter a slump or a tough loss, curiosity helps you ask, "What can I learn from this?" rather than "Why did this happen to me?" This approach transforms disappointment into data and frustration into fuel for growth, making you both mentally tougher and more adaptable.

 Actionable Insight: After your next loss or tough practice, write down three things the experience taught you. Use these lessons to set a small, specific goal for your next session.

September 19
THE HUMILITY TO LEARN FROM ALL

> "Be slow in considering, but resolute in action."
> — BIAS OF PRIENE (STOIC-ADJACENT, QUOTED BY SENECA)

A curious mind is humble enough to learn from anyone — coach, peer, or even a less experienced player. The Stoics valued careful consideration before decisive action. In tennis, this means observing others, asking questions, and weighing advice before you make changes. Once you decide, commit fully. This blend of humility and resolve ensures you're always learning, but never paralyzed by indecision. It's how you turn curiosity into real improvement.

Actionable Insight: Watch a teammate or opponent closely in your next session. Notice one thing they do well that you don't. Ask them about it, and try incorporating their advice into your practice.

September 20
CURIOSITY AS A DAILY PRACTICE

> "Apply yourself both to present circumstances and to those ahead. The present time is enough for you."
> — Marcus Aurelius

Curiosity is not a one-time event but a daily practice. The Stoics taught the importance of being attentive to the present while preparing for the future. In tennis, this means approaching every session with fresh eyes — looking for new details, patterns, or sensations in your game. By making curiosity a habit, you ensure that every day on court brings an opportunity for discovery and growth, no matter how routine it may seem.

 Actionable Insight: Before each practice this week, set a curiosity goal: What's one thing I want to notice or learn today? At the end of the session, jot down your discovery and how it might shape your next steps.

September 21
CURIOSITY AND THE ART OF NOTICING

> "Nothing escapes the notice of the vigilant mind."
> — SENECA

Curiosity is sharpened by your willingness to notice the small details others overlook. The Stoics believed that a vigilant mind is always observing, always learning, always alert for the subtle cues that can make the difference between victory and defeat. In tennis, this means paying attention to the way your opponent tosses the ball, the sound of your strings, or the shift in your own emotions during a match. When you train yourself to notice more, you gain an edge that goes beyond skill — you become a student of the game in every sense. This habit of noticing not only improves your tennis but also deepens your appreciation for the sport and your own progress.

Actionable Insight: During your next practice or match, pick one detail to observe closely — your opponent's footwork, your own breathing, or the rhythm of the rallies. Write down what you notice and how it might inform your next steps.

September 22
THE POWER OF ASKING FOR HELP

> "Do not be ashamed to ask for help. Even the greatest minds have needed guidance."
>
> — Seneca

Curiosity is humble enough to admit when it doesn't know. The Stoics remind us that learning is a communal process — no one grows alone. In tennis, asking for help from a coach, teammate, or even an opponent is not a sign of weakness, but of wisdom. By seeking guidance, you open yourself up to new perspectives and accelerate your development. This willingness to learn from others not only improves your game but also builds stronger relationships and a supportive community around you.

 Actionable Insight: This week, ask someone you respect for feedback on a specific part of your game. Listen carefully, thank them, and try to apply at least one piece of their advice in your next session.

September 23
FIND JOY IN THE PROCESS OF DISCOVERY

"Joy is found not in finishing an activity but in doing it."
— GREG ANDERSON (STOIC-ADJACENT)

The Stoics teach that fulfillment comes from the process, not just the outcome. In tennis, the real joy is in the act of discovery — trying a new grip, learning a new tactic, or finally understanding a piece of advice that never clicked before. When you focus on the process of learning rather than just the result, you find satisfaction in every step, no matter how small. This attitude keeps you motivated through setbacks and helps you appreciate the journey as much as the destination.

Actionable Insight: In your next session, set a process-oriented goal: "Today I will experiment with my serve toss," or "I will focus on my recovery steps." At the end, reflect on what you enjoyed and what you discovered, regardless of your win/loss record.

September 24
CURIOSITY FOSTERS CREATIVITY

> "Nothing is so conducive to innovation as a mind free from preconceptions."
> — MARCUS AURELIUS (PARAPHRASED)

Creativity in tennis is born from curiosity — the willingness to try new strategies, invent new routines, and see familiar situations with fresh eyes. The Stoics believed that a mind unburdened by rigid expectations is open to inspiration and innovation. By questioning the status quo and experimenting with new ideas, you keep your game dynamic and unpredictable. This not only makes you a tougher opponent but also keeps your passion for tennis alive.

 Actionable Insight: In your next practice, deliberately try a new pattern of play or an unconventional shot. Notice how it feels and what results it brings. Reflect on how curiosity can lead to creative breakthroughs.

September 25
THE COURAGE TO BE A PERPETUAL STUDENT

> "True wisdom comes to each of us when we realize how little we understand about life, ourselves, and the world around us."
>
> — SOCRATES (STOIC-ADJACENT)

The greatest athletes and thinkers never stop learning. The Stoics valued the humility to remain a student, no matter how much you achieve. In tennis, this means always being open to feedback, new techniques, and even radical change. The courage to admit you don't know everything is what keeps you growing long after others have plateaued. It's this mindset that transforms good players into great ones, and keeps the game fresh for a lifetime.

 Actionable Insight: After your next match, write down one thing you still don't fully understand about your game. Make a plan to explore it through study, coaching, or experimentation this week.

September 26
CURIOSITY AND THE WISDOM OF PATIENCE

> "Patience is the key to joy."
> — Rumi (Stoic-adjacent, widely referenced by Stoic writers)

Curiosity must be paired with patience. The Stoics knew that meaningful answers and real improvement take time to emerge. In tennis, you may not see immediate results from your experiments or questions, but patience allows your discoveries to take root. By giving yourself time to absorb new lessons and let changes settle, you avoid the frustration that comes from rushing the process. Patience and curiosity together ensure that your learning is deep and lasting.

Actionable Insight: Pick one aspect of your game you're curious about and commit to exploring it patiently for the next week. Track your progress and remind yourself that true growth is gradual.

September 27
TURN SETBACKS INTO CURIOSITY

> "Failure is simply the opportunity to begin again, this time more intelligently."
>
> — HENRY FORD (STOIC-ADJACENT)

Setbacks are inevitable, but the Stoic-curious mind sees them as invitations to learn. When you lose a match or struggle with a skill, ask "What can I try differently next time?" instead of "Why did I fail?" This approach transforms disappointment into motivation and keeps your journey moving forward. Every setback is a chance to ask better questions, develop new strategies, and become a more resilient player.

Actionable Insight: After your next setback, write down three questions: What happened? What can I learn? What will I try next? Use these answers to guide your next practice.

September 28
CURIOSITY STRENGTHENS RELATIONSHIPS

"Associate with those who will make a better man of you."
— SENECA

Curiosity isn't just about self-improvement — it's also about learning from others. The Stoics encouraged seeking out wise companions and mentors. In tennis, this means surrounding yourself with people who challenge you, inspire you, and help you see your blind spots. By being curious about others' experiences and perspectives, you expand your own understanding and accelerate your growth. These relationships become a source of support, motivation, and wisdom throughout your journey.

Actionable Insight: Reach out to a teammate, coach, or even a friendly rival and ask about their training routines or mindset. See what you can learn from their approach and consider how it might benefit your own.

September 29
CURIOSITY AND THE PRACTICE OF REFLECTION

> "The unexamined life is not worth living."
> — SOCRATES

Reflection is the natural companion of curiosity. The Stoics and their philosophical kin believed that regularly examining your thoughts, actions, and results is essential for growth. In tennis, this means taking time after each match or practice to ask what went well, what didn't, and why. Reflection turns experience into wisdom and ensures that your curiosity leads to lasting improvement rather than endless wandering. It's through honest self-examination that you turn questions into answers and setbacks into stepping stones.

 Actionable Insight: After your next session, spend five minutes reflecting on one thing you learned about your game, your mindset, or your habits. Write it down and set a small goal based on your insight.

September 30
CURIOSITY AS A WAY OF LIFE

> "Wonder is the beginning of wisdom."
> — Socrates

The Stoic-curious life is one of perpetual wonder. When you greet each day, each match, and each challenge with a sense of curiosity, you keep your mind open and your spirit eager to grow. This approach transforms tennis — and life — into an endless adventure, where every experience is a chance to learn, adapt, and become wiser. Curiosity is not a phase, but a practice that sustains your passion and progress for a lifetime.

Actionable Insight: Begin each day this week by asking yourself: "What can I discover today?" Carry this sense of wonder onto the court, and let it inspire your play, your practice, and your interactions with others.

September Wrap-Up: Strategic Thinking — Wisdom Between the Lines

This month, you shifted from reacting to **responding with strategy**. In tennis, instincts matter — but without intention behind them, they can become scattered efforts. September was about learning how to play smarter: anticipating instead of guessing, solving problems mid-match, and using your mind as your most effective weapon.

The Stoics taught that reason is our highest faculty — and in tennis, this shows up in how you prepare, how you adapt, and how you make choices under pressure. You've explored how to analyze patterns, manage momentum, and make adjustments when your Plan A falls short. You've practiced **observing without judgment**, seeing clearly, and acting deliberately.

Smart tennis isn't just about knowing tactics — it's about emotional discipline paired with logic. It's taking time to pause between points, check in with your breath, and ask: *What's working? What's needed?* Strategic players don't just hit — they **think**, **read**, and **adjust**. They win not just with power, but with presence.

October

The Discipline of Purpose – Aligning Action with Values

O CTOBER IS ABOUT intentional living — on and off the court. The Stoics, like top tennis players, understood that drifting through life or play without a clear purpose leads to frustration and wasted effort. This month, you'll learn to set your course with clarity, align your actions with your values, and design each day with purpose. In tennis, as in life, success isn't accidental; it's the result of deliberate choices, disciplined routines, and a vision for where you want to go. This is the month to stop playing on autopilot and start living — and playing — by design.

October 1
LIVE BY DESIGN, NOT DEFAULT

> "If you do not know to which port you are sailing, no wind is favorable."
>
> — Seneca

Without a clear goal or plan, even the best effort can be wasted. In tennis, showing up to practice without intention leads to aimless hitting and slow progress. The Stoics remind us that purpose gives meaning to every action. When you know your destination — whether it's mastering your serve or building mental toughness — every drill and match becomes a step toward that goal. Living by design means making conscious choices about your training, your mindset, and your reactions, rather than letting circumstances or emotions dictate your path.

Actionable Insight: Before your next session, set a specific intention: What do you want to improve? How will you measure success today? Write down your "port" — your goal for the month — and revisit it daily to keep your course steady.

October 2
DEFINE THE WORTH OF YOUR AMBITION

> "A man's worth is no greater than the worth of his ambitions."
> — Marcus Aurelius

Your goals reveal your values. What you aim for — titles, self-improvement, consistency, legacy — shapes the way you train, compete, and grow. Marcus Aurelius reminds us that ambition isn't inherently virtuous — it's the *kind* of ambition that determines your character. In tennis, are you chasing validation, or are you pursuing mastery and integrity? When your ambitions are aligned with your deeper purpose, your performance becomes more focused, resilient, and meaningful. Your worth as a competitor grows in direct proportion to the clarity and honor of your goals.

 Actionable Insight: Write down your top 1–2 ambitions in tennis. Then ask: *What do these ambitions say about me?* Refine one of them to reflect a higher value — something intrinsic, like excellence, resilience, or respect. Make that your north star for the month.

October 3
SET INTENTIONAL GOALS

> "Life without a design is erratic."
> — SENECA

Wandering through practice without goals is like sailing without a map. The Stoics and elite athletes alike know that specific, intentional goals channel your energy and focus. Whether it's improving your backhand or managing nerves under pressure, clarity about your aims transforms random effort into progress. Goals give you direction and motivation, especially on tough days.

Actionable Insight: Set one process-based goal for your next week of tennis (e.g., "I will focus on footwork during every rally"). Track your progress and adjust your plan as needed.

October 4
DESIGN YOUR ROUTINE

"Excellence is not an act, but a habit."

— ARISTOTLE

Champions are built through daily routines, not occasional bursts of effort. The Stoics believed that habits shape character. In tennis, a well-designed routine — warm-up, mental preparation, post-match reflection — creates consistency and resilience. When you design your day with intention, you reduce decision fatigue and make it easier to act in alignment with your goals.

 Actionable Insight: Review your current tennis routine. Identify one habit to add or improve this week (e.g., a five-minute visualization before matches). Notice how intentional routines impact your performance.

October 5
ACT WITH PURPOSE

> "Waste no more time arguing what a good man should be. Be one."
>
> — MARCUS AURELIUS

Purposeful action separates the disciplined from the distracted. The Stoics urge us to stop theorizing and start living our values. On the court, this means approaching every drill, point, and match with intention and effort — not just going through the motions. When you act with purpose, you build confidence, skill, and character.

Actionable Insight: Before each practice or match, ask yourself: "What is my purpose today?" Remind yourself of this intention whenever you feel your focus slipping.

October 6
REVIEW AND ADJUST YOUR COURSE

"Self-examination is the key to insight."

— SOCRATES

No plan survives contact with reality unchanged. The Stoics and top athletes review their progress regularly, adjusting their course as needed. In tennis, this means reflecting after each session: What worked? What needs improvement? Regular review keeps you aligned with your goals and prevents drift.

 Actionable Insight: After each practice this week, spend five minutes journaling: What did I do well? Where did I stray from my plan? Use these insights to refine your approach for tomorrow.

October 7
FOCUS ON WHAT YOU CONTROL

> "It is not in our control to have everything turn out exactly as we want, but it is in our control to control how we respond to what happens."
>
> — EPICTETUS

On the tennis court, you can't dictate your opponent's skill, the weather, or the outcome of every point. What you can always control is your response — your attitude, your effort, and your focus. Epictetus reminds us that while external events are unpredictable, your reactions are entirely within your power. When you accept this, frustration fades and you play with greater freedom. Instead of wasting energy on bad calls or unlucky bounces, channel it into your next shot and your next decision. This mindset not only builds resilience but also helps you stay present and perform at your best, regardless of circumstances.

 Actionable Insight: During your next match or practice, whenever something outside your control happens — like a bad bounce or a questionable line call — pause and remind yourself: "I control my response." Use that moment to reset, refocus, and give your best effort on the very next point.

October 8
LIVE EACH DAY BY DESIGN

"Concentrate every minute like a Roman — like a man — on doing what's in front of you with precise and genuine seriousness... stop being aimless."

— Marcus Aurelius

Living by design is a daily practice, not a one-time decision. The Stoics remind us that every moment is a chance to act with purpose. On the court, this means giving full attention to each point, each drill, each opportunity to improve. Over time, these moments of intention add up to mastery.

Actionable Insight: At the start of each day, set a clear intention for your tennis and your life. Review this intention at the end of the day, celebrating moments when you lived by design rather than default.

October 9
LOOK WITHIN FOR DIRECTION

> "Look within. Within is the fountain of good, and it will ever bubble up, if thou wilt ever dig."
> — Marcus Aurelius

The greatest source of clarity and purpose isn't found in external validation, but in honest self-reflection. In tennis, it's tempting to look to coaches, rankings, or peers for direction, but true growth begins by turning inward and asking what you truly want from your game. The Stoics remind us that your inner values and motivations are the wellspring of all meaningful progress. When you regularly reflect on your intentions and desires, you align your actions with your deepest goals, making your journey more authentic and rewarding. This introspection empowers you to play — and live — with conviction, regardless of outside pressures.

 Actionable Insight: Set aside five minutes after practice to journal about your motivations for playing tennis. Ask yourself: "What do I want from this journey?" Let your answers guide your training and competition this week.

October 10
MASTER YOURSELF TO FIND FREEDOM

> "No man is free who is not master of himself."
> — Epictetus

Self-mastery is the foundation of both Stoic philosophy and athletic excellence. In tennis, freedom on the court comes not from talent alone, but from discipline over your thoughts, emotions, and habits. The Stoics teach that true liberty is achieved by mastering your impulses — choosing your responses rather than reacting automatically. When you control your focus, your routines, and your attitude, you unlock the ability to play your best under any circumstances. This self-control not only improves your performance but also builds confidence that you can handle whatever the match brings.

 Actionable Insight: Identify one area where you tend to lose self-control during matches (e.g., frustration, rushing points). This week, practice pausing and resetting whenever you notice this impulse.

October 11
LET EVERY EFFORT HAVE AN END IN VIEW

> "Let all your efforts be directed to something, let it keep that end in view. It's not activity that disturbs people, but false conceptions of things that drive them mad."
>
> — SENECA

Purposeful action is the antidote to frustration and burnout. In tennis, it's easy to fall into the trap of "busywork" — endless drills or matches without clear intention. The Stoics warn that activity without a guiding purpose leads to confusion and dissatisfaction. By setting a clear end for each practice or match, you ensure that your energy is channeled toward meaningful progress. This focus not only accelerates improvement but also brings greater satisfaction, as every effort serves a larger goal.

 Actionable Insight: Before each practice, write down one specific outcome you want to achieve. At the end, review whether your actions aligned with that goal.

October 12
PROGRESS IS BUILT ON DAILY PRACTICE

"Progress is not achieved by luck or accident, but by working on yourself daily."

— Epictetus

Improvement in tennis — and in life — isn't the result of sudden breakthroughs, but of steady, consistent effort. The Stoics remind us that daily practice, even when results aren't immediately visible, is the surest path to growth. Every session, every drill, every point played with intention adds up over time. This commitment to daily work builds resilience, skill, and confidence, making you a more formidable competitor and a stronger person.

 Actionable Insight: Commit to one small, specific practice habit this week (e.g., 10 minutes of serves each day). Track your consistency and reflect on your progress after seven days.

October 13
THE POWER OF SAYING NO

> "It may take some hard work. But the more you say no to the things that don't matter, the more you can say yes to the things that do."
>
> — THE DAILY STOIC

Discipline isn't just about what you do — it's also about what you choose not to do. In tennis, distractions abound: social media, negative self-talk, or unproductive routines can all sap your focus and energy. The Stoics teach that saying "no" to what doesn't serve your purpose frees you to fully commit to what does. By eliminating distractions, you create space for deeper practice, better recovery, and more meaningful progress. This selective focus is a hallmark of champions.

Actionable Insight: Identify one distraction that commonly interferes with your tennis goals. For the next week, consciously say "no" to it and use that time or energy to reinforce a positive habit.

October 14
FOCUS ON WHAT YOU CAN CONTROL

"Do not waste time on what you cannot control."
— Marcus Aurelius

The Stoic dichotomy of control is a powerful tool for athletes. In tennis, many factors — opponents, weather, line calls — are outside your influence. The Stoics urge us to focus only on what we can change: our effort, our preparation, our mindset. By letting go of what's beyond your reach, you conserve energy and reduce frustration, allowing you to perform at your highest level. This focus on controllables is the foundation of mental toughness and consistent performance.

 Actionable Insight: Before your next match, list three things you can control and three you cannot. Whenever you feel distracted by the uncontrollable, redirect your attention to your own actions.

October 15
TRUE HAPPINESS IS FOUND IN THE PRESENT

> "True happiness is to enjoy the present, without anxious dependence upon the future, not to amuse ourselves with either hopes or fears but to rest satisfied with what we have, which is sufficient, for he that is so wants nothing."
> — SENECA

It's easy to become preoccupied with future results or past regrets, but the Stoics remind us that fulfillment is found in the present moment. In tennis, this means immersing yourself fully in each point, each rally, each breath. When you rest in the present, you play with greater freedom, clarity, and joy. This presence not only improves your performance but also deepens your appreciation for the game itself.

 Actionable Insight: During your next practice, use a simple cue (like bouncing the ball before a serve) to anchor yourself in the present. Whenever your mind wanders, gently bring it back to the current point.

October 16
DISCIPLINE IS THE BRIDGE TO ACCOMPLISHMENT

> "Small disciplines repeated with consistency every day lead to great achievements gained slowly over time."
> – John C. Maxwell

Greatness in tennis isn't built overnight — it's the result of small, consistent acts of discipline. The Stoics and modern thinkers alike recognize that daily habits, not occasional bursts of effort, create lasting success. Whether it's sticking to your warm-up routine, practicing your weakest shot, or maintaining a positive mindset, these small disciplines compound over time. Each day you choose discipline, you move one step closer to your goals.

 Actionable Insight: Choose one small discipline to add to your daily tennis routine (e.g., stretching after practice). Track your consistency for the rest of the month and notice the cumulative impact.

October 17
THE KEY TO CONTROL IS YOUR OWN MIND

> "The key to control is not in controlling external events, but in controlling your own mind."
>
> — Epictetus

External events in tennis — bad calls, tough draws, unexpected challenges — are unpredictable. The Stoics teach that your true power lies in mastering your thoughts and reactions. By training your mind to remain calm, focused, and adaptable, you maintain control even when circumstances are chaotic. This inner mastery is the hallmark of resilient athletes and wise individuals alike, enabling you to respond thoughtfully rather than react impulsively.

Actionable Insight: During your next match, notice when your mind starts to spiral due to external events. Pause, take a deep breath, and consciously choose your response.

October 18
DO LESS, BUT DO IT BETTER

> "If you seek tranquility, do less. Or (more accurately) do what's essential — what the reason of a social being requires, and in the requisite way. Which brings a double satisfaction: to do less, better."
> — Marcus Aurelius

Quality always trumps quantity. In tennis, it's easy to overtrain or spread your effort across too many areas, but the Stoics advocate for focusing on what's truly essential and doing it well. By simplifying your routines and concentrating on key priorities, you reduce stress and increase your effectiveness. This approach leads to deeper learning, greater satisfaction, and more consistent improvement.

 Actionable Insight: Review your current tennis schedule. Identify one area where you can do less but with greater focus and quality. Notice how this shift affects your performance and mindset.

October 19
YOUR THOUGHTS SHAPE YOUR EXPERIENCE

> "The happiness of your life depends upon the quality of your thoughts. Take control of what you think about."
> — Marcus Aurelius

Your mindset is the lens through which you experience every match, practice, and challenge. The Stoics remind us that by choosing constructive, empowering thoughts, you elevate not only your performance but also your enjoyment of the game. Negative thinking leads to frustration and self-doubt, while positive, purposeful thoughts build resilience and confidence. The quality of your thoughts is a skill you can train, just like your serve or footwork.

 Actionable Insight: After each practice, reflect on one positive thought that helped you during the session. Make it a habit to consciously choose your thoughts before and during matches.

October 20
DON'T WAIT TO DEMAND THE BEST FOR YOURSELF

> "How long are you going to wait before you demand the best for yourself?"
>
> — Epictetus

The Stoics challenge us to take responsibility for our own growth and excellence. In tennis, it's easy to wait for the "right" coach, the perfect conditions, or a lucky break, but real progress begins when you decide to give your best — right now. By holding yourself to higher standards and taking initiative, you accelerate your improvement and build self-respect. This proactive mindset transforms your approach to every practice and match.

 Actionable Insight: Set one ambitious, specific goal for your tennis this week. Take the first step today, no matter how small, and commit to pursuing your best effort every day.

October 21
REVIEW AND REFLECT FOR CONTINUOUS GROWTH

> "I will keep constant watch over myself and — most usefully — will put each day up for review. For this is what makes us evil — that none of us looks back upon our own lives."
> — SENECA

Self-reflection is the engine of progress. The Stoics and elite athletes alike understand that honest review of your actions, decisions, and mindset is essential for continuous growth. In tennis, this means not just playing matches, but actively analyzing what went well, what didn't, and how you can improve. This habit of daily review helps you spot patterns, correct mistakes, and reinforce positive behaviors, ensuring that every experience becomes a stepping stone to mastery.

 Actionable Insight: After each practice or match this week, spend five minutes journaling: What did I do well? Where can I improve? Use these insights to set a goal for your next session.

October 22
LET PURPOSE GUIDE YOUR ACTIONS

> "Your purpose in life is to find your purpose and give your whole heart and soul to it."
>
> — BUDDHA (STOIC-ALIGNED)

A clear sense of purpose is a powerful motivator. In tennis, knowing why you play — whether for joy, growth, competition, or connection — fuels your commitment and resilience. The Stoics and other wisdom traditions teach that when you give your full heart to a meaningful purpose, setbacks become easier to bear and victories more fulfilling. Purpose transforms routine practice into passionate pursuit and mundane matches into meaningful milestones.

 Actionable Insight: Write down your core purpose for playing tennis. Keep it visible in your gear bag or locker, and revisit it whenever you need motivation or clarity.

October 23
ACCEPT WHAT YOU CANNOT CHANGE

> "Freedom is the only worthy goal in life. It is won by disregarding things that lie beyond our control."
> — Epictetus

True freedom on the court — and in life — comes from letting go of the need to control everything. The Stoics teach that by accepting what you cannot change, you liberate yourself from frustration and anxiety. In tennis, this means embracing the unpredictability of matches, the imperfections of your game, and the reality of external circumstances. Acceptance isn't resignation; it's the gateway to focused, empowered action on what truly matters.

Actionable Insight: Before your next match, make a conscious decision to accept whatever comes — good or bad. Whenever you feel resistance, remind yourself that freedom lies in focusing on your response, not the outcome.

October 24
EMBODY YOUR PHILOSOPHY

"Don't explain your philosophy. Embody it."

– Epictetus

Actions speak louder than words. The Stoics urge us to live our values, not just talk about them. In tennis, this means demonstrating sportsmanship, resilience, and effort in every drill, every match, every interaction. When you embody your philosophy, you inspire others and build a reputation of integrity and strength. This consistency between belief and action is the mark of both great athletes and wise individuals.

 Actionable Insight: Choose one Stoic principle (e.g., composure, discipline, gratitude) to embody during your next match. Reflect afterward on how living your values affected your experience and performance.

October 25
SURROUND YOURSELF WITH UPLIFTING PEOPLE

> "The key is to keep company only with people who uplift you, whose presence calls forth your best."
> — Epictetus

Your environment shapes your progress as much as your effort. The Stoics advise us to seek out relationships and communities that challenge, support, and inspire us. In tennis, training with positive, driven teammates and coaches accelerates your growth and keeps you motivated. Conversely, negative influences can sap your energy and undermine your confidence. Choose your circle wisely, and let their example elevate your own standards.

Actionable Insight: Reflect on the people you spend the most time with in your tennis life. Identify one person who uplifts and inspires you, and make a plan to spend more time learning from them this month.

October 26
LISTEN MORE THAN YOU SPEAK

"We have two ears and one mouth so that we can listen twice as much as we speak."

— Epictetus

Listening is a powerful tool for learning and connection. The Stoics remind us that wisdom comes from paying attention — to coaches, to opponents, to your own body and mind. In tennis, being a good listener means absorbing feedback, observing patterns, and staying open to new ideas. This humility and curiosity accelerate your improvement and deepen your understanding of the game.

Actionable Insight: During your next lesson or practice, focus on listening intently to your coach or partner. Afterward, write down one new thing you learned by being attentive.

October 27
BE CONTENT TO BE THOUGHT A BEGINNER

> "If you want to improve, be content to be thought foolish and stupid."
>
> — EPICTETUS

Growth requires vulnerability. The Stoics teach that the path to mastery often involves looking awkward, making mistakes, and risking embarrassment. In tennis, this means being willing to try new techniques, ask questions, and accept feedback, even if it exposes your weaknesses. Embracing the discomfort of being a beginner is the gateway to real progress and lasting confidence.

Actionable Insight: This week, deliberately work on a weakness, even if it feels uncomfortable or exposes your inexperience. Embrace the awkwardness as evidence that you're on the path to improvement.

October 28
THE FOUNTAIN OF GOOD IS WITHIN

> "Look well into thyself; there is a source of strength which will always spring up if thou wilt always look."
> — MARCUS AURELIUS

In tennis, it's tempting to search for confidence in external things — new gear, a coach's praise, or a winning streak. But Marcus Aurelius reminds us that the true wellspring of strength, resilience, and goodness lies within. When you face a tough opponent or a challenging match, remember: your ability to reset, refocus, and fight for every point comes from your own inner resources. The more you trust in your preparation, your values, and your mindset, the more you'll find that the power to persevere and play your best is always available — no matter the score or the circumstances.

Actionable Insight: Before your next match, take a quiet moment to reflect on your past efforts and growth. Remind yourself that everything you need to compete with courage and integrity is already inside you. When the pressure mounts, look within for the strength to respond with your best tennis.

October 29
CURB YOUR DESIRES

> "Curb your desire — don't set your heart on so many things and you will get what you need."
> — Epictetus

Desire can be motivating, but unchecked, it leads to frustration and disappointment. The Stoics teach that by moderating your wants, you find contentment and focus. In tennis, this means letting go of the need for constant wins, perfect conditions, or recognition. When you focus on the essentials — effort, learning, growth — you free yourself from unnecessary anxiety and play with greater ease and satisfaction.

Actionable Insight: Before your next match, notice any desires or expectations you're holding onto. Practice letting them go, and commit to playing for the love of the game itself.

October 30
THE WISDOM OF SMALL STEPS

> "Well-being is realized by small steps, but is truly no small thing."
>
> – Zeno

Lasting progress is built on incremental improvements. The Stoics remind us that each small step — each practice, each adjustment, each lesson — compounds into significant change over time. In tennis, focusing on daily improvement rather than instant results keeps you motivated and resilient, even through setbacks. Celebrate every bit of progress, knowing that greatness is the result of countless small victories.

Actionable Insight: At the end of this month, reflect on one small improvement you've made in your game. Acknowledge your progress and set a new small goal for the coming month.

October 31
LIVE BY DESIGN, REFLECT BY DESIGN

> "An unexamined life is not worth living."
> — SOCRATES (STOIC-ADJACENT)

As October closes, the Stoics remind us that intentional living requires regular reflection. In tennis, as in life, reviewing your journey — your choices, your growth, your setbacks — ensures that you continue to live and play by design, not default. This habit of self-examination keeps your purpose clear, your actions aligned, and your progress steady. By reflecting on your month, you honor your commitment to growth and set the stage for even greater achievements ahead.

Actionable Insight: Take time today to review your month: What did you learn? How did you live by design? Write down one lesson and one intention for November.

October Wrap-Up: Tennis by Design

THIS MONTH, YOU learned to approach tennis with intention — setting clear goals, building purposeful routines, and aligning your actions with your values each time you stepped on court. The Stoics and tennis champions alike know that excellence comes from daily discipline, not luck or accident. As you move forward, keep steering your tennis journey by design, not default: focus on what you can control, adjust your course when needed, and let each practice and match reflect your chosen purpose. No matter how the winds of competition shift, a clear vision and steady habits will keep your game — and your mindset — on track.

November Theme

The Virtue of Generosity — Giving and Growing Through Tennis

NOVEMBER IS DEDICATED to generosity — not just in giving to others, but in sharing your time, effort, encouragement, and spirit on and off the court. The Stoics saw generosity as a sign of inner strength and abundance. In tennis, generosity means supporting your peers, sharing knowledge, and playing with an open heart. This month, you'll discover how giving freely can deepen your growth and enrich your tennis journey.

November 1
THE GIFT OF ENCOURAGEMENT

> "He who gives liberally goes not without reward."
> — Seneca

A kind word or gesture can uplift a teammate or even an opponent. The Stoics remind us that generosity is not just material — it's encouragement, support, and the willingness to help others succeed. In tennis, your encouragement can transform someone's confidence and create a positive environment. Generosity of spirit builds stronger teams and friendships, and it often comes back to you in unexpected ways.

Actionable Insight: Today, give genuine encouragement to a peer — praise their effort, celebrate their improvement, or offer support after a tough point. Notice how this generosity affects both of you.

November 2
SHARE WHAT YOU'VE LEARNED

> "Light tomorrow with today."
> — Elizabeth Barrett Browning
> (Stoic-adjacent)

Your experiences — both victories and defeats — are valuable not just for you, but for those around you. The Stoics believed that wisdom grows when it is shared. In tennis, passing along what you've learned helps others avoid pitfalls and accelerates their growth. Sharing knowledge is an act of generosity that strengthens the entire community.

 Actionable Insight: Offer one piece of advice or share a lesson you've learned with a less experienced player. Reflect on how teaching reinforces your own understanding.

November 3
GENEROSITY IN COMPETITION

> "Compete with yourself, not with others."
> — MARCUS AURELIUS
> (PARAPHRASED)

True generosity in sport means playing to raise the level of the game, not just to defeat others. The Stoics teach us to focus on self-improvement rather than comparison. In tennis, this means giving your best effort and respecting your opponent's effort as well. When you compete to bring out the best in yourself and others, you foster mutual growth and enjoyment.

Actionable Insight: In your next match, focus on playing your best tennis, regardless of the score. Acknowledge your opponent's good shots and effort, and reflect on how this mindset changes your experience.

November 4
THE ABUNDANCE OF GRATITUDE

> "Gratitude is not only the greatest of virtues, but the parent of all the others."
>
> — Cicero
> (Stoic-adjacent)

Generosity begins with gratitude. When you appreciate what you have — your health, your ability to play, your support system — you naturally want to give back. The Stoics saw gratitude as a wellspring of kindness and generosity. In tennis, a grateful attitude makes you more likely to support others, share your time, and play with joy.

Actionable Insight: List three things about your tennis journey you are grateful for. Consider how you can "pay it forward" to others in your tennis community this week.

November 5
GIVING TIME

> "Time is a gift, given to you, given to give you the time you need, the time you need to have the time of your life."
> — Norton Juster
> (Stoic-adjacent)

One of the most generous things you can offer is your time — whether it's hitting balls with a beginner, volunteering at an event, or simply listening to a teammate. The Stoics valued the wise use of time as one of life's greatest treasures. Giving your time to others not only helps them, but enriches your own experience and deepens your sense of purpose.

Actionable Insight: Volunteer to help someone with their game or assist at a tennis event this week. Reflect on how giving your time changes your perspective on your own journey.

November 6
GENEROSITY IN DEFEAT

> "Be gracious in defeat and humble in victory."
>
> — Unknown
> (Stoic-adjacent)

How you handle loss is as important as how you handle victory. The Stoics taught that character is revealed in adversity. In tennis, being generous in defeat means congratulating your opponent, learning from the match, and offering encouragement. This grace builds respect and strengthens the tennis community.

 Actionable Insight: After your next loss, sincerely congratulate your opponent and reflect on what you learned. Notice how this generosity of spirit helps you move forward.

November 7
THE STRENGTH TO FORGIVE

> "To forgive is to set a prisoner free and discover the prisoner was you."
>
> — Lewis B. Smedes
> (Stoic-adjacent)

Holding onto grudges — against opponents, partners, or yourself — only weighs you down. The Stoics believed in releasing resentment to maintain inner peace. In tennis, forgiveness allows you to move on from mistakes and conflicts, freeing your energy for growth and connection.

Actionable Insight: Identify one grudge or lingering frustration in your tennis life. Make a conscious effort to let it go, and observe how this act of generosity toward yourself or others lightens your mind.

November 8
SHARING JOY

> "Joy shared is joy doubled."
>
> — Proverb
> (Stoic-adjacent)

Celebrating your own successes is important, but sharing in the joy of others magnifies happiness for all. The Stoics valued community and the collective pursuit of virtue. In tennis, cheering for a friend's breakthrough or celebrating a teammate's win creates a supportive, uplifting atmosphere.

Actionable Insight: This week, celebrate someone else's achievement — big or small. Let their joy inspire you and notice how sharing in their happiness enhances your own.

November 9
THE GENEROSITY OF ATTENTION

> "Attention is the rarest and purest form of generosity."
> — SIMONE WEIL
> (STOIC-ADJACENT)

Giving someone your undivided attention is one of the most generous acts you can offer. In tennis, this means truly listening to your coach, noticing your partner's needs, and being present for your teammates. When you focus fully on others, you foster trust and connection, making your tennis community stronger and more supportive. Attention is a gift that costs nothing but means everything.

Actionable Insight: In your next practice, put away distractions and give your full attention to your coach or partner. Notice how this deepens your learning and strengthens your relationships.

November 10
GENEROSITY IN SHARING THE SPOTLIGHT

"Success is best when it's shared."

— Howard Schultz
(Stoic-adjacent)

Generosity means celebrating others' achievements as much as your own. In tennis, this is the spirit of doubles partners who lift each other up, or teammates who cheer for every win. Sharing the spotlight not only builds camaraderie but also reminds you that every victory is a team effort, whether seen or unseen.

Actionable Insight: After your next match, highlight something your partner or teammate did well. Let them know their effort is noticed and appreciated.

November 11
THE GENEROSITY OF SECOND CHANCES

> "The greatest gift you can give another is the purity of your attention."
>
> — RICHARD MOSS
> (STOIC-ADJACENT)

Everyone makes mistakes, but not everyone is offered a second chance. The Stoics teach us to be generous in forgiveness and patience. In tennis, this means allowing your partner, or even yourself, to recover from errors without blame. Second chances foster growth, trust, and resilience — qualities that benefit the whole team.

Actionable Insight: When a partner or opponent makes a mistake, offer encouragement instead of criticism. Notice how this generosity lifts the mood and performance of everyone involved.

November 12
GIVING WITHOUT EXPECTATION

> "Do not do to others what angers you if done to you by others."
>
> — Isocrates
> (Stoic-adjacent)

True generosity expects nothing in return. The Stoics believed that virtue is its own reward. In tennis, this means offering help, advice, or support simply because it's the right thing to do. When you give freely, you create a positive environment that benefits everyone, including yourself.

 Actionable Insight: This week, help a fellow player — pick up extra balls, offer a tip, or lend an ear — without expecting anything back. Reflect on how this act of generosity feels.

November 13
THE GENEROSITY OF HONEST FEEDBACK

> "Only the educated are free."
> — Epictetus

Honest feedback is a gift that helps others grow. The Stoics valued truth spoken kindly. In tennis, constructive criticism — offered with respect — can accelerate improvement for your peers and yourself. Generosity in feedback is about wanting the best for others, not about pointing out flaws.

Actionable Insight: Ask a teammate if they'd like feedback on their game. Offer one positive observation and one suggestion for growth, and invite them to do the same for you.

November 14
THE GENEROSITY OF PATIENCE

"Patience is the art of concealing your impatience."
— Guy Kawasaki
(Stoic-adjacent)

Patience is a subtle but powerful form of generosity. The Stoics knew that growth takes time, and that patience with others' learning curves is a gift. In tennis, waiting for a beginner to master a drill or for a partner to find their rhythm is a way of supporting their journey. Your patience creates a safe space for others to improve.

 Actionable Insight: During your next group session, practice patience when someone struggles. Offer encouragement and remember your own learning process.

November 15
GENEROSITY IN SHARING OPPORTUNITY

> "Opportunity is missed by most people because it is dressed in overalls and looks like work."
>
> — Thomas Edison
> (Stoic-adjacent)

Generosity sometimes means creating or sharing opportunities — inviting a new player to join a match, recommending a teammate for a tournament, or sharing practice time. By helping others seize opportunities, you foster a spirit of abundance and growth in your tennis circle.

Actionable Insight: Invite someone new to join your practice or match this week. Notice how sharing opportunity benefits both of you.

November 16
THE GENEROSITY OF ENCOURAGEMENT

> "Encouragement is oxygen to the soul."
> — George M. Adams
> (Stoic-adjacent)

A word of encouragement can make all the difference in a tough match or practice. The Stoics knew that lifting others up is a sign of inner strength. In tennis, your encouragement can help a partner recover from mistakes or inspire a teammate to keep pushing.

Actionable Insight: Offer specific encouragement to someone struggling this week — acknowledge their effort or improvement, and see how it impacts their spirit.

November 17
THE GENEROSITY OF FORGIVING YOURSELF

> "To forgive oneself is to begin to love oneself."
> — JOHN PAUL II
> (STOIC-ADJACENT)

Self-forgiveness is an act of generosity that frees you from the weight of past mistakes. The Stoics taught that everyone errs, but growth comes from learning and moving forward. In tennis, forgiving your own errors allows you to play with renewed confidence and joy.

Actionable Insight: After your next mistake, pause, forgive yourself, and focus on the next point. Notice how this self-generosity helps you recover faster.

November 18
GENEROSITY IN ADVERSITY

> "In prosperity, it is very easy to find a friend; but in adversity, it is the most difficult of all things."
> — Epictetus

True generosity is revealed when times are tough. The Stoics believed that supporting others in adversity is the mark of a virtuous person. In tennis, being there for a teammate after a loss or during a slump shows the strength of your character and the depth of your community.

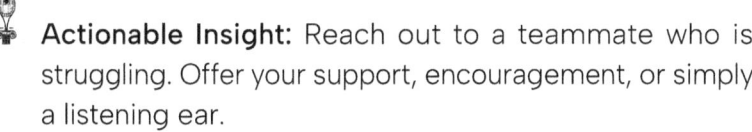 **Actionable Insight:** Reach out to a teammate who is struggling. Offer your support, encouragement, or simply a listening ear.

November 19
THE GENEROSITY OF LETTING GO

"Let go, or be dragged."

— Zen Proverb
(Stoic-adjacent)

Sometimes the most generous thing you can do is let go — of grudges, mistakes, or the need to be right. The Stoics taught that clinging to the past only causes suffering. In tennis, letting go frees you to focus on the present and play with joy.

Actionable Insight: After each match, consciously release any lingering frustration or disappointment. Write it down, then let it go.

November 20
GENEROSITY IN CELEBRATING OTHERS

> "Rejoice with those who rejoice."
>
> — Paul the Apostle
> (Stoic-adjacent)

Celebrating others' successes is a generous act that builds community and trust. The Stoics valued the ability to find joy in others' happiness. In tennis, this means applauding a rival's improvement or congratulating a teammate on a win, even if you fell short.

- **Actionable Insight:** This week, make it a point to celebrate someone else's achievement, big or small. Notice how this generosity uplifts both of you.

November 21
GENEROSITY OF SPIRIT

> "A generous heart, kind speech, and a life of service and compassion are the things which renew humanity."
> — BUDDHA
> (STOIC-ADJACENT)

Generosity of spirit is about more than actions — it's about the attitude you bring to every interaction. The Stoics believed that kindness and compassion are at the heart of virtue. In tennis, a generous spirit transforms competition into camaraderie and rivals into friends.

Actionable Insight: Approach your next match with the intention to be generous in spirit — win or lose, focus on kindness, encouragement, and respect.

November 22
THE GENEROSITY OF SHARING SUCCESS

"There is no delight in owning anything unshared."

— Seneca

Success is sweeter when shared. The Stoics taught that joy multiplies when celebrated with others. In tennis, this means involving your team, family, or supporters in your victories, acknowledging their role in your journey.

 Actionable Insight: After your next success, thank those who helped you get there. Share the celebration and reflect on the power of teamwork.

November 23
THE GENEROSITY OF TEACHING

> "Teaching is the highest form of understanding."
> — ARISTOTLE (STOIC-ADJACENT)

Sharing what you know is an act of generosity that deepens your own mastery. The Stoics valued teaching as a way to reinforce wisdom. In tennis, mentoring a younger player or explaining a tactic helps both of you grow.

Actionable Insight: Offer to teach a skill or drill to a less experienced player this week. Notice how teaching clarifies your own understanding.

November 24
THE GENEROSITY OF A LISTENING EAR

> "To listen well is as powerful a means of communication and influence as to talk well."
> — John Marshall (Stoic-adjacent)

Sometimes, the most generous thing you can do is simply listen. The Stoics valued the power of attentive listening. On the court, being there for a teammate or friend who needs to talk builds trust and strengthens bonds.

Actionable Insight: This week, make time to listen — really listen — to a teammate or friend. Offer your attention without judgment or advice.

November 25
GENEROSITY IN SHARING THE SPOTLIGHT

> "Great leaders don't set out to be a leader... they set out to make a difference. It's never about the role — always about the goal."
>
> — LISA HAISHA
> (STOIC-ADJACENT)

Generosity means sharing the spotlight and giving others a chance to shine. The Stoics believed in serving the greater good over personal glory. In tennis, celebrate your partner's or teammate's achievements and support their moments of success.

 Actionable Insight: In your next doubles match or team event, highlight your partner's strengths and celebrate their successes as much as your own.

November 26
THE GENEROSITY OF LETTING OTHERS LEAD

> "A wise man learns more from his enemies than a fool from his friends."
>
> — NIKI LAUDA
> (STOIC-ADJACENT)

Sometimes, generosity means stepping back and letting others take the lead. The Stoics valued humility and the willingness to learn from anyone. In tennis, allowing a partner to call the plays or a teammate to take charge can foster growth and teamwork.

 Actionable Insight: In your next group practice or match, let someone else lead a drill or make strategic decisions. Reflect on what you learn from their approach.

November 27
THE GENEROSITY OF HONEST PRAISE

> "Praise, like gold and diamonds, owes its value only to its scarcity."
>
> — SAMUEL JOHNSON
> (STOIC-ADJACENT)

Genuine praise is a powerful motivator. The Stoics valued honesty and authenticity, and sincere praise can inspire others to reach new heights. In tennis, recognizing a teammate's progress or an opponent's skill fosters mutual respect and encourages continued effort.

Actionable Insight: Offer specific, honest praise to someone today — focus on a real improvement or effort you've noticed.

November 28
THE GENEROSITY OF LETTING GO OF CREDIT

> "It is amazing what you can accomplish if you do not care who gets the credit."
>
> — Harry S. Truman
> (Stoic-adjacent)

Generosity sometimes means letting go of the need for recognition. The Stoics taught that true virtue is its own reward. In tennis, focus on the team's success, not personal accolades. When you care more about the group than your own ego, everyone rises.

Actionable Insight: In your next team event, contribute fully without seeking recognition. Reflect on how this generosity affects your satisfaction and your team's results.

November 29
THE GENEROSITY OF SHARING JOY

> "Shared joy is a double joy; shared sorrow is half a sorrow."
> — Swedish Proverb
> (Stoic-adjacent)

Joy multiplies when shared. The Stoics believed that community and connection are essential for a flourishing life. In tennis, celebrating victories and supporting each other through losses makes the journey richer and more meaningful for everyone involved.

Actionable Insight: Celebrate a teammate's win or comfort them after a loss. Notice how sharing emotions — both high and low — strengthens your bond.

November 30
THE GENEROSITY OF GRATITUDE

"Gratitude turns what we have into enough."

— Aesop
(Stoic-adjacent)

Generosity and gratitude are intertwined. The Stoics taught that appreciating what you have opens the door to giving more. In tennis, gratitude for your opportunities, teammates, and progress inspires you to give back and share your joy.

 Actionable Insight: At the end of this month, write a thank-you note to someone who has supported your tennis journey. Express your gratitude and reflect on how giving thanks enriches your life.

November Wrap-Up: The Virtue of Generosity — Giving and Growing Through Tennis

THIS MONTH, YOU explored how giving makes you stronger — not weaker. In tennis, generosity isn't just about compliments or good sportsmanship — it's in the **extra ball you feed your partner**, the **encouragement you offer after a tough point**, or the **honest call you make even when it costs you**.

The Stoics taught that true generosity comes from inner abundance, not scarcity. And on court, that means sharing what you've learned, competing with integrity, and showing respect even in heated moments. You discovered that lifting others doesn't lower your game — it raises the standard for everyone, including you.

You played not just to win, but to connect. You gave your full effort regardless of the crowd, the score, or the stakes. That's generosity in action: **offering your best, freely and without ego**.

As you head into the final month, remember this — every match is a chance to give: your focus, your respect, your full presence. And in giving, you grow.

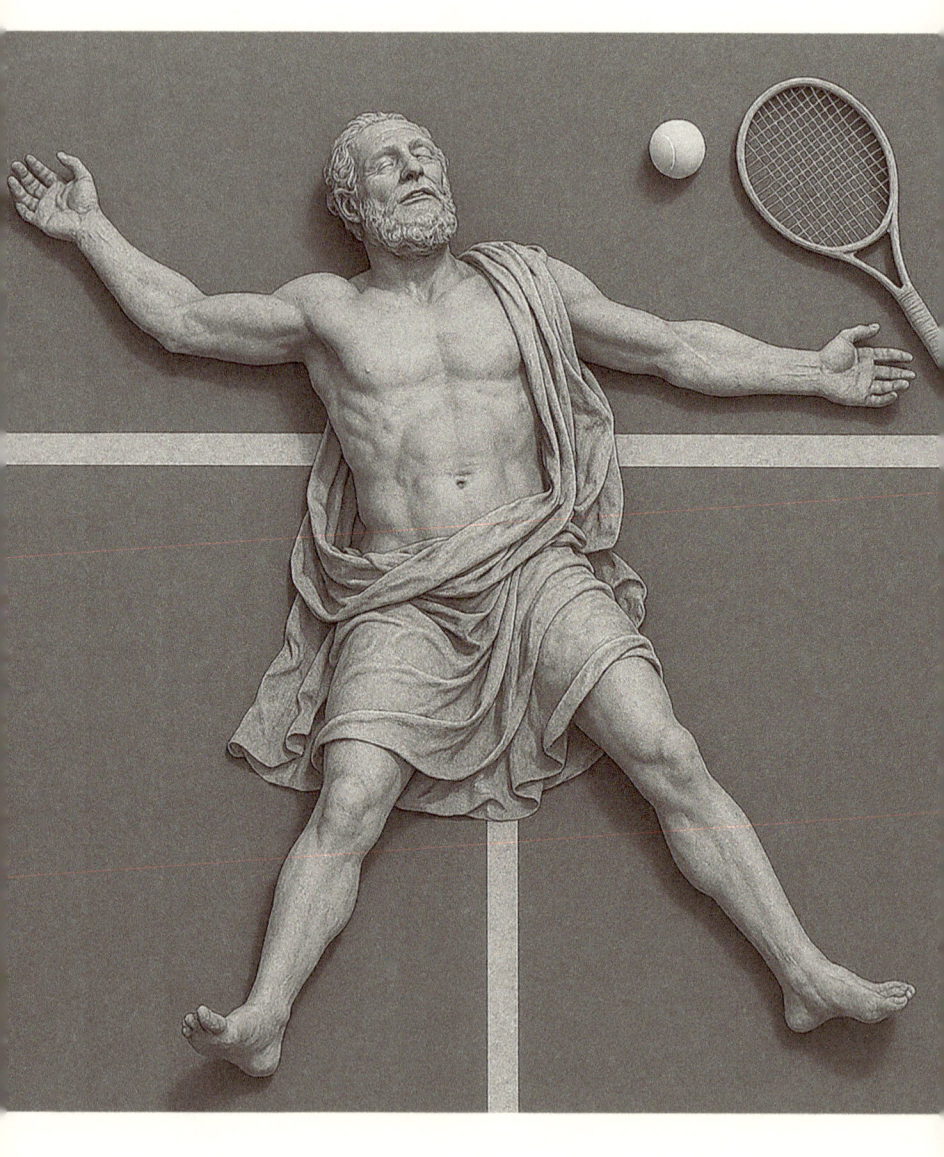

December Theme

The Virtue of Reflection — Wisdom Gained, Lessons Carried Forward

December is dedicated to reflection — the Stoic practice of reviewing your journey, extracting wisdom from experience, and preparing for the year ahead. In tennis, reflection means honest self-assessment, celebrating growth, and setting new intentions. This month, you'll use the power of reflection to finish strong and lay the groundwork for greater mastery in the new year.

December 1
THE VALUE OF LOOKING BACK

> "Life can only be understood backwards; but it must be lived forwards."
> — SØREN KIERKEGAARD
> (STOIC-ADJACENT)

Reflection is the bridge between experience and wisdom. The Stoics believed that reviewing your actions and choices is essential for growth. In tennis, looking back at your season — your wins, losses, and lessons — helps you understand what worked, what didn't, and why. This honest review is not about regret, but about learning and preparing for what's next.

Actionable Insight: Spend 10 minutes today reviewing your tennis year. Write down your three biggest lessons and one area you want to focus on next.

December 2
CELEBRATE GROWTH, NOT JUST RESULTS

"Progress is not in enhancing what is, but in advancing toward what will be."

— Kahlil Gibran
(Stoic-adjacent)

The Stoics remind us that true progress is measured by growth, not just results. In tennis, it's easy to get caught up in wins and losses, but real success lies in how much you've learned and improved. Celebrate the steps you've taken, the skills you've gained, and the resilience you've built. This focus on growth keeps you motivated and optimistic for the future.

 Actionable Insight: Write down one area where you've made progress this year, no matter how small. Share it with a coach or friend and celebrate the journey.

December 3
THE WISDOM OF HONEST SELF-ASSESSMENT

> "An honest man is always a child."
>
> — SOCRATES
> (STOIC-ADJACENT)

Honesty with yourself is the foundation of improvement. The Stoics valued self-assessment as a path to virtue and mastery. In tennis, this means evaluating your strengths and weaknesses without ego or self-criticism. Honest reflection allows you to set realistic goals and make meaningful changes. It's not about being harsh, but about being truthful and open to growth.

Actionable Insight: After your next match, rate yourself in three areas: technical skill, mental focus, and sportsmanship. Identify one area to work on this month.

December 4
LEARN FROM EVERY EXPERIENCE

> "Experience is the teacher of all things."
> — Julius Caesar
> (Stoic-adjacent)

Every match, practice, and conversation is a lesson waiting to be learned. The Stoics believed that wisdom comes from attentive experience. In tennis, reflecting on each experience — good or bad — turns every moment on court into a stepping stone for growth. By learning from everything, you ensure that no effort is wasted.

Actionable Insight: After each session this week, write down one thing you learned — about your game, your mindset, or yourself. Share your insight with a coach or teammate to reinforce your learning.

December 5
THE POWER OF LETTING GO

> "Letting go gives us freedom, and freedom is the only condition for happiness."
>
> — THICH NHAT HANH
> (STOIC-ADJACENT)

Reflection is not just about remembering — it's about releasing what no longer serves you. The Stoics taught that holding onto regrets, grudges, or past mistakes only weighs you down. In tennis, letting go of a tough loss or a missed opportunity frees you to focus on the present and the future. This act of release is a gift you give yourself, opening space for new growth.

Actionable Insight: Identify one regret or frustration from this year. Write it down, acknowledge it, and then let it go. Notice how this lightens your mindset for the matches ahead.

December 6
THE PRACTICE OF DAILY REVIEW

> "Let each thing you would do, say, or intend be like that of a dying person."
>
> — Marcus Aurelius

The Stoics advocated for daily review as a way to keep your actions aligned with your values. In tennis, ending each day with a brief reflection — what you did well, what you'd change, and what you're grateful for — keeps your journey purposeful and your progress steady.

 Actionable Insight: Tonight, spend five minutes reviewing your tennis day. What are you proud of? What will you do differently tomorrow?

December 7
THE WISDOM OF LEARNING FROM OTHERS

> "By three methods we may learn wisdom: First, by reflection, which is noblest; Second, by imitation, which is easiest; and third by experience, which is the bitterest."
>
> — CONFUCIUS
> (STOIC-ADJACENT)

Reflection includes learning from others' journeys, not just your own. The Stoics believed in seeking wisdom wherever it could be found. In tennis, observe great players, listen to coaches, and learn from your peers. Their experiences can accelerate your own growth.

 Actionable Insight: Watch a match or read about a player you admire. Reflect on one lesson you can apply to your own tennis.

December 8
THE STRENGTH TO CHANGE COURSE

"Change is never painful, only the resistance to change is painful."

— BUDDHA
(STOIC-ADJACENT)

Reflection sometimes reveals the need to change direction. The Stoics taught that adapting to new information is a strength, not a weakness. In tennis, being willing to adjust your training, tactics, or mindset keeps you moving forward, even when the path shifts.

Actionable Insight: Review your routines this week. Is there something you've outgrown? Make one change to better align with your current goals.

December 9
THE JOY OF REMEMBERING WHY

> "Remember why you started."
>
> — Unknown
> (Stoic-adjacent)

Reflection isn't just about improvement — it's about reconnecting with your original motivation. The Stoics valued clarity of purpose. In tennis, remembering why you play — love of the game, the challenge, the community — reinvigorates your passion and guides your decisions.

Actionable Insight: Write down your original reason for playing tennis. Revisit it before your next match and let it inspire your effort and attitude.

December 10
THE GIFT OF CLOSURE

> "Every ending is a new beginning."
>
> — Proverb
> (Stoic-adjacent)

The end of a season, a partnership, or a tournament can be bittersweet. The Stoics taught that closure is necessary for growth. In tennis, reflecting on endings allows you to celebrate what was, learn from it, and move forward with intention.

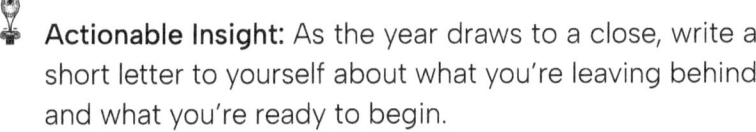 **Actionable Insight:** As the year draws to a close, write a short letter to yourself about what you're leaving behind and what you're ready to begin.

December 11
THE WISDOM OF ACCEPTANCE

> "Acceptance of what has happened is the first step to overcoming the consequences of any misfortune."
> — WILLIAM JAMES
> (STOIC-ADJACENT)

Acceptance is the foundation of reflection. The Stoics taught that only by accepting reality can you begin to change it. In tennis, accepting your results — good or bad — frees you to focus on what you can improve.

Actionable Insight: After your next match, accept the outcome without judgment. Focus your energy on what you'll do next, not what you wish had happened.

December 12
THE REFLECTIVE POWER OF SOLITUDE

> "In solitude the mind gains strength and learns to lean upon itself."
>
> — Laurence Sterne
> (Stoic-adjacent)

Solitude is a powerful tool for reflection. The Stoics valued time alone to think, plan, and recover. In tennis, quiet moments after practice or a match help you process emotions, set new goals, and recharge for the next challenge.

Actionable Insight: Take a solitary walk after your next match or practice. Use the time to reflect on your performance and set one intention for improvement.

December 13
THE WISDOM OF GRATITUDE

> "Gratitude is not only the greatest of virtues, but the parent of all others."
>
> — Cicero
> (Stoic-adjacent)

Reflection deepens gratitude. The Stoics taught that recognizing your blessings fosters humility, joy, and generosity. In tennis, gratitude for your opportunities, coaches, and teammates sustains your motivation and enriches your journey.

Actionable Insight: Make a gratitude list for your tennis year. Share it with someone who supported you along the way.

December 14
THE POWER OF PERSPECTIVE

"We can complain because rose bushes have thorns, or rejoice because thorns have roses."

— ALPHONSE KARR
(STOIC-ADJACENT)

Reflection is about choosing your perspective. The Stoics believed that how you frame your experiences shapes your reality. In tennis, focus on the positives — the lessons learned, the friendships made, the progress achieved — rather than the setbacks.

 Actionable Insight: After your next loss or disappointment, write down three positives you can take from the experience.

December 15
THE GIFT OF SETTING NEW INTENTIONS

> "The best way to predict the future is to create it."
> — ABRAHAM LINCOLN
> (STOIC-ADJACENT)

Reflection is most powerful when it leads to action. The Stoics encouraged setting intentions based on honest review. In tennis, use your reflections to set new goals, refine your routines, and approach the coming year with purpose.

Actionable Insight: Set one clear, actionable goal for your tennis in the new year. Write it down and outline the first step you'll take to achieve it.

December 16
THE STRENGTH OF SELF-COMPASSION

> "Be kind, for everyone you meet is fighting a hard battle."
> — Ian Maclaren
> (Stoic-adjacent)

Reflection is not about harsh self-judgment, but about compassionate self-awareness. The Stoics taught that kindness, including to yourself, is essential for growth. In tennis, treat yourself with the same patience and encouragement you'd offer a friend.

 Actionable Insight: After your next mistake, pause and offer yourself a kind word. Notice how self-compassion helps you recover and refocus.

December 17
THE WISDOM OF LETTING OTHERS IN

> "Shared joy is a double joy; shared sorrow is half a sorrow."
> — Swedish Proverb
> (Stoic-adjacent)

Reflection is richer when shared. The Stoics valued community and mutual support. In tennis, discussing your experiences with teammates or coaches provides new insights and strengthens your bonds.

Actionable Insight: Share a reflection from your tennis year with a friend or mentor. Invite them to share theirs, and learn from each other's journeys.

December 18
THE POWER OF FORGIVENESS

> "To err is human; to forgive, divine."
>
> — Alexander Pope
> (Stoic-adjacent)

Forgiveness is essential for moving forward. The Stoics taught that holding onto resentment, whether toward yourself or others, blocks growth. In tennis, forgiving mistakes — your own and others' — frees you to play with joy and confidence.

Actionable Insight: Identify one mistake or slight you're holding onto. Practice forgiveness and notice how it lightens your mood and improves your focus.

December 19
THE WISDOM OF HUMILITY

> "True humility is not thinking less of yourself; it is thinking of yourself less."
>
> — C.S. Lewis
> (Stoic-adjacent)

Reflection fosters humility. The Stoics taught that recognizing your limitations is the first step to wisdom. In tennis, humility keeps you open to learning, receptive to feedback, and grounded in your pursuit of mastery.

Actionable Insight: After your next win, reflect on what you still have to learn. Thank someone who helped you along the way.

December 20
THE STRENGTH TO BEGIN AGAIN

"Every day is a chance to begin again."

— Buddha
(Stoic-adjacent)

Reflection is not just about looking back — it's about starting fresh. The Stoics believed in the power of renewal. In tennis, each practice, each match, and each point is a new opportunity to improve and enjoy the game.

Actionable Insight: Before your next session, set a small intention for something you want to do differently. Embrace the chance to begin again.

December 21
THE WISDOM OF SIMPLICITY

"Simplicity is the ultimate sophistication."
— Leonardo da Vinci
(Stoic-adjacent)

Reflection helps you strip away the unnecessary and focus on what matters. The Stoics valued simplicity as a path to clarity and peace. In tennis, simplifying your routines, strategies, and goals allows you to play with greater composure and effectiveness.

Actionable Insight: This week, identify one area of your tennis life that feels complicated. Simplify it — whether it's your warm-up, your game plan, or your mindset.

December 22
THE GIFT OF ANTICIPATION

"Anticipation is the purest form of pleasure."
— Vladimir Nabokov
(Stoic-adjacent)

Reflection is not just about the past — it's about looking forward with hope and excitement. The Stoics taught that wise anticipation prepares you for challenges and opportunities. In tennis, looking ahead to new goals and adventures keeps your passion alive.

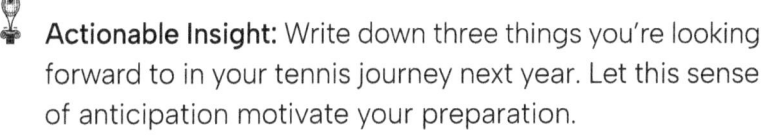 **Actionable Insight:** Write down three things you're looking forward to in your tennis journey next year. Let this sense of anticipation motivate your preparation.

December 23
THE WISDOM OF BALANCE

> "Balance is not something you find, it's something you create."
>
> — Jana Kingsford
> (Stoic-adjacent)

Reflection helps you find balance — between effort and rest, ambition and contentment, competition and camaraderie. The Stoics taught that a well-balanced life is a happy one. In tennis, balance allows you to sustain your progress and enjoy the journey.

Actionable Insight: Review your tennis schedule. Are you balancing training, rest, and fun? Make one change to create better balance this week.

December 24
THE JOY OF CELEBRATION

> "Celebrate what you want to see more of."
> — Tom Peters
> (Stoic-adjacent)

Reflection is a time to celebrate your wins, big and small. The Stoics believed in acknowledging progress and savoring joy. In tennis, celebrating your achievements reinforces positive habits and keeps your motivation high.

Actionable Insight: Today, celebrate a recent accomplishment — no matter how minor. Share your success with someone who supports you.

December 25
THE GIFT OF PRESENCE

> "Wherever you are, be all there."
>
> — Jim Elliot
> (Stoic-adjacent)

Presence is the greatest gift you can give yourself and others. The Stoics valued being fully engaged in the moment. In tennis, presence means letting go of distractions and immersing yourself in the game, the community, and the joy of play.

Actionable Insight: During your next session, put away your phone and other distractions. Focus completely on the court, your partner, and the experience.

December 26
THE WISDOM OF CONTENTMENT

> "Contentment is natural wealth."
>
> — SOCRATES
> (STOIC-ADJACENT)

Reflection brings contentment by helping you appreciate what you have. The Stoics taught that true wealth is found in being satisfied with enough. In tennis, contentment allows you to enjoy the game, your progress, and your relationships, without constant striving.

Actionable Insight: List three things about your tennis life that bring you contentment. Reflect on how this sense of enough supports your happiness.

December 27
THE STRENGTH TO DREAM

> "Go confidently in the direction of your dreams."
> — Henry David Thoreau
> (Stoic-adjacent)

Reflection is a launching pad for new dreams. The Stoics believed in the pursuit of excellence and purpose. In tennis, daring to dream — of new skills, new achievements, new adventures — keeps you inspired and moving forward.

Actionable Insight: Set a bold tennis dream for the coming year. Write it down and share it with someone who will encourage you.

December 28
THE GIFT OF CLOSURE

> "Closure is the art of letting go and moving on."
> — Unknown
> (Stoic-adjacent)

As the year ends, reflection helps you find closure — on matches, seasons, or relationships. The Stoics taught that moving on is essential for peace and progress. In tennis, closure frees you to embrace new challenges with a clear mind and open heart.

Actionable Insight: Reflect on something you're ready to close the door on. Write about it, thank it for what it taught you, and let it go.

December 29
THE WISDOM OF HOPE

> "Hope is the companion of power, and mother of success."
> — SAMUEL SMILES
> (STOIC-ADJACENT)

Reflection fuels hope for the future. The Stoics saw hope as a virtue that sustains effort and ambition. In tennis, hope keeps you training, competing, and believing in your potential, even after setbacks.

Actionable Insight: Write down one hope for your tennis journey next year. Let it guide your preparation and inspire your actions.

December 30
THE POWER OF NEW BEGINNINGS

> "Every new beginning comes from some other beginning's end."
>
> — SENECA

The end of the year is the perfect time to reflect, release, and prepare for a new start. The Stoics believed that every ending is also a beginning. In tennis, this means carrying forward your lessons, letting go of regrets, and stepping into the new year with purpose and enthusiasm.

Actionable Insight: Write a letter to your future self about what you want to carry forward and what you want to leave behind. Read it before your first match of the new year.

December 31
THE WISDOM OF COMPLETION

> "Finish each day and be done with it. You have done what you could."
>
> — Ralph Waldo Emerson
> (Stoic-adjacent)

Reflection is complete when you can let go of the past and rest in the knowledge that you gave your best. The Stoics taught that peace comes from doing your duty and then releasing attachment to outcomes. In tennis, as in life, the ability to finish each day, each match, and each year with satisfaction and acceptance is the true measure of success.

Actionable Insight: Tonight, reflect on your tennis year. Celebrate your effort, forgive your mistakes, and let go of what's done. Rest, recharge, and prepare to begin again.

December Wrap-Up: The Virtue of Reflection — Wisdom Gained, Lessons Carried Forward

THIS MONTH, YOU slowed down — not to stop, but to look back with clarity. The Stoics believed that reflection turns experience into wisdom. In tennis, that means reviewing not just your wins and losses, but your mindset, habits, and growth over time.

You learned to ask the deeper questions: *How did I compete? Where did I grow? What still needs work?* You saw that progress isn't always in the scoreline — it's in the way you carry yourself after a tough loss, or how you bounce back from a rough set. You discovered that reflection isn't self-criticism — it's self-awareness in motion.

Just as you analyze a match to prepare for the next one, reflection helps you end the year with intention, not just momentum. You celebrate what worked, learn from what didn't, and begin planning how to rise even higher.

Because mastery isn't a straight line — it's a cycle of play, review, and renewal. And now, you're ready to begin again — wiser, stronger, and more focused than ever.

www.ingramcontent.com/pod-product-compliance
Lightning Source LLC
Chambersburg PA
CBHW032145080426
42735CB00008B/596